HEADINGLEY

'THIS PLEASANT RURAL VILLAGE'

CLUES TO THE PAST

BY EVELEIGH BRADFORD

ROYALTIES FROM THE SALE OF THIS BOOK WILL BE DONATED TO
THE HEADINGLEY DEVELOPMENT TRUST FOR THE 'HEART' PROJECT
(HEADINGLEY ENTERPRISE AND ARTS CENTRE).

Published by Northern Heritage Publications
an imprint of Jeremy Mills Publishing Limited
www.jeremymillspublishing.co.uk

First published 2008
Text © Eveleigh Bradford 2008
Images © as attributed

ISBN 978–1–906600–32–7 (paperback)
ISBN 978–1–906600–37–2 (hardback)

Cover Image
Headingley village around 1810 (artist unknown).
(Thoresby Society)

Frontispiece
'The Skyrack Oak, Headingley, in Winter, 1830'
by Joseph Rhodes. The old oak, reputedly dating
back to Anglo-Saxon times, is shown here as already
aged and decaying. The cottage behind it was later
converted into a bank and rebuilt. The large house
on the right, known as Oak House, survived into the
1920s, used as a dairy and shop for farm produce.
(©Leeds Museums and Galleries)

CONTENTS

TOPICS

Maps

ACKNOWLEDGEMENTS
MAPS AND ILLUSTRATIONS

The 1711 Cardigan Estate Map is reproduced by kind permission of the Hon. Mr. E. Brudenell of Deene Park.

The 1846 Tithe Commissioners' Map of Headingley-cum-Burley is reproduced by permission of the National Archives, Kew.

The 1908 Ordnance Survey Map, sheet 203.13, is reproduced by permission of the Trustees of the National Library of Scotland.

The author is grateful to the following bodies for permission to reproduce images from their collections (credits are given under the images concerned):

The Thoresby Society
Leeds Library and Information Services
Leeds Museums and Galleries
Leeds University
Leeds University Special Collections
The Leeds Library
West Yorkshire Archive Service
The Royal Geographical Society

All images without a credit are from the author's own collection.

NOTES ON SOME OF THE
ARTISTS/ILLUSTRATORS FEATURED

Joseph Rhodes (1782–1854) was born in Leeds, studied at the Royal Academy in London, and then returned to Leeds where he set up his own art school. He tutored several well-known Leeds artists, exhibited locally, and painted a number of Leeds scenes, many of which are in the Leeds Art Gallery collection.

John N. Rhodes (1809–1842) was Joseph Rhodes' son. He too went to London to work and exhibited twice at the Royal Academy before returning to Leeds, where he died aged only 33. A talented and admired artist, his health was undermined by heavy drinking. He painted a number of Yorkshire country and local scenes. (See W.H.Thorp, *John N.Rhodes, A Yorkshire Painter 1809–1842*, Leeds, 1904.)

Walter Braithwaite (1852–1920?) was a Leeds artist and photographer, who lived for many years at 8 Monk Bridge Road, Headingley, and had a studio in town. He made a number of drawings and paintings of local scenes, including around his home in Headingley, in the late nineteenth century, some of them evocations of the past. Several of his drawings are in the collection of Leeds Local Studies Library, others with the Thoresby Society, of which he was a member.

W. R. Robinson (William Ripley Robinson, artist and drawing master, Fenton Street, Leeds) was a painter of landscapes and local scenes, active in Leeds in the 1840s. He was commissioned by the antiquarian William Boyne to provide several pictures for his personal copy of Whitaker's *Loidis and Elmete*, which Boyne enhanced with many additional illustrations. Boyne's seven-volume edition is now in the collection of the Leeds Local Studies Library and is one of its treasures.

Godfrey Bingley (1842–1927) was a well-known and prolific amateur photographer who lived all his life in Headingley, though he travelled widely. When his sight began to fail, he donated his extensive, carefully-catalogued collection of glass slides and negatives, covering a wide range of subjects including the neighbourhood of his home, to Leeds University where it is now in the Special Collections of the Library. (John E. Jones, 'A Noble Gift', *University of Leeds Review*, Vol. 30, 1987/88.)

ABBREVIATIONS

WYAS	West Yorkshire Archive Service
NRO	Northamptonshire Record Office
LLS Library	Leeds Local Studies Library
Th.Soc.	Thoresby Society
PThS	Publications of the Thoresby Society
YAS	Yorkshire Archaeological Society
YAJ	Yorkshire Archaeological Journal

'THIS PLEASANT RURAL VILLAGE'

THAT IS HOW Edward Parsons described Headingley in his history of Leeds, published in 1834.[1] It was still a country village, separated from the town by the expanse of Woodhouse Moor and by the fields and farms which bordered the narrow, rutted lane leading from the Moor over the hill down to the village. An old, low chapel stood on the village green, and next to it a small charity school. Two inns faced them across the road, and round about there were scattered cottages and houses, and fields of crops and pasture land. Along the lane to the north, a smithy and a small brewery and tannery were working; and beyond the village, near the handsome parsonage, stretched the rough, open moor where cattle and sheep could roam, with a mill down by the beck. There were already some signs of change. Parsons noted that the village was beginning to show the effects of the growth and prosperity of nearby Leeds, offering a rural retreat for wealthy merchants who could afford to build their 'mansions and elegant villas' there, away from the increasingly polluted atmosphere of the town. He could not foresee how quickly, as the long reign of Queen Victoria began, the village would be transformed. Within a few years the wild moor and the rest of the common land was divided up and fenced off for development; the small, ancient chapel was demolished and a tall, spacious

1. E. Parsons, *The Civil, Ecclesiastical, Literary, Commercial and Miscellaneous History of Leeds*, Leeds, 1834.

church built in its place; the school was rebuilt and
extended; the roads were improved and an omnibus service
to town introduced; and, in the quiet fields nearby,
an ambitious new tourist attraction, the Zoological and
Botanical Gardens, opened to the public, bringing hordes
of visitors. The following decades were to see the creation
of new streets, the building of fine villas and terraces, and
the development of the village into 'the most fashionable
suburb' of the town. Towards the end of the century there
was a further shift as close-packed brick terraces began to
crowd over former gardens and pleasure grounds, filling
the remaining spaces and giving the village the varied
character it retains today. This process of change and
development during the nineteenth century is the focus of
this book.

History shapes what we see around us, and everywhere
there are traces of the past which it is easy to pass by
without much thought – buildings, maybe used for new
purposes; walls and gateposts; lanes and paths; names of
places and roads. Clues visible to anyone taking a stroll
within a half-mile radius of St Michael's Church or the
Original Oak pub provided the starting point for the
studies which follow in this book. But to understand the
clues, it helps to look back at the historical context.

For most people nowadays Headingley is simply a
name for a neighbourhood, one of the many suburbs of
Leeds, though with its own well-recognised identity and
character. The focus is the cluster of shops, cafes and other
buildings between the Original Oak pub, the Arndale
Centre, and the bottom of North Lane, next to the cricket
ground which has made the name of Headingley familiar
in distant corners of the world. This heart-shaped area was
the core of the village as long ago as 1711 when the first
map of the area was drawn up, but its origins lie further
back still.

The name Headingley, first recorded in Domesday
Book, originally referred to a much larger area than the
village itself. From the Norman Conquest until the
nineteenth century Headingley (later known as Headingley-

cum-Burley) had a distinct and separate identity in several contexts: as a manor, with its own manorial administration; as a chapelry within the ancient, vast Parish of Leeds; and as a township, the largest of the ten 'out-townships' clustered round the central township of Leeds itself. It covered an area of some 3,000 acres, stretching from the edge of Woodhouse Moor out to the borders of Adel and Horsforth, and from the River Aire across to Meanwood Beck. The area contained large expanses of woodland at Weetwood and Hawksworth, a stretch of wild moorland called Headingley Moor, and the prominent feature of the steep-sided, wooded Ridge. There were villages at Burley and Kirkstall as well as the village of Headingley itself, and a small settlement at Far Headingley, on the northern fringe of the Moor.

From the seventeenth century onwards the township was part of the Borough of Leeds and subject to governance by the Corporation. Inevitably it was bound by social and economic ties to the inner township, but it retained a measure of administrative independence well into the nineteenth century. In the early 1830s, when Parsons was writing, it still raised its own highway and poor rates, held 'town meetings' to discuss local issues and to appoint the local constable and surveyors of the highways, and retained the old manorial court, the Court Baron. But all this was gradually to change during the course of the century.[2]

The history of Headingley village is inevitably bound up with the history of the manor and township, and the various families which, with Kirkstall Abbey, have been Lords of the Manor and owners of the land. The next chapter looks back on this story.

---

2. Following municipal reform in 1835, the township became a ward of the Borough with elected representatives on the Council. Thus it was drawn closer into the life of the Borough, gradually losing its independent functions. See B.J.Barber, 'Municipal Government in Leeds, 1835–1914', in D.Fraser, ed., *Municipal Reform and the Industrial City*, Leicester, 1982; and R.J.Morris, *Class, Sect and Society: The Making of the British Middle Class, Leeds 1820–1850*, Manchester, 1990.

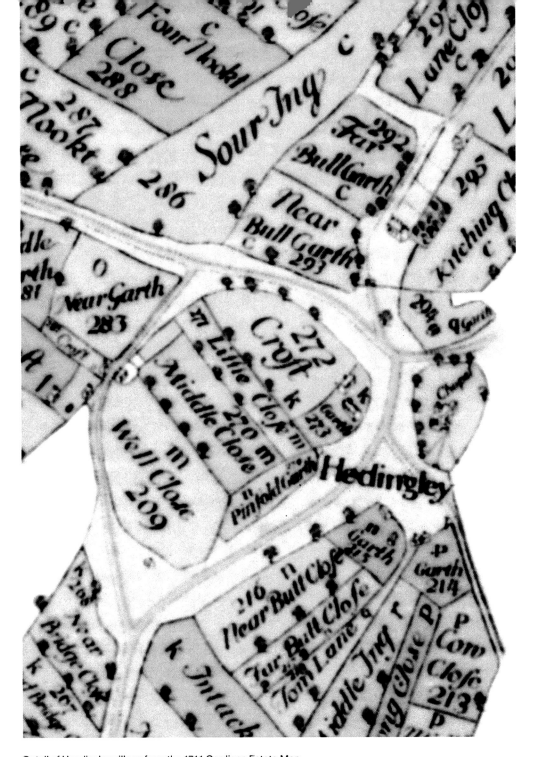

Detail of Headingley village from the 1711 Cardigan Estate Map.
The chapel is shown, and a number of houses, the largest being Headingley Hall (not named) with its orchard and 'kitching close' (kitchen garden) and a farmhouse or barn behind. Eleven other scattered houses are indicated. Fields fill the triangle between the three (unnamed) roads: one leading southwards to Kirkstall (now St Michael's Road/Kirkstall Lane), one leading northwest towards Adel and Otley (the Otley Road), the third (North Lane) linking the two. All are bordered by areas of 'waste' or common land. There are only two other roads: the lane coming in from Leeds in the east (Headingley Lane), and Chapel Lane to the southeast, leading up to the chapel from Burley village. *(Reproduced by permission of the Hon. Mr. E. Brudenell)*

LORDS, LANDS, AND THE ABBEY

THE NAME HEADINGLEY is more than a thousand years old. It pre-dates the Norman Conquest in 1066 and is probably Anglian in origin, from that period in the ninth and tenth centuries when the Angles and the Danes fought over the possession of the land. Various interpretations of the name have been suggested, the most common being 'the field (ley) of the sons of Haedda'. There was a Danish chieftain called Haedda (or Hed or Hadda), known to have been killed around the year 901, but the name more probably belongs to an earlier leader of Anglian origin. Whatever the truth, the name has survived to identify the place and link it with its distant past.

DOMESDAY BOOK

The first written record of Headingley, as for so many other English settlements, is in Domesday Book, compiled in 1086 on the instructions of William the Conqueror, who sent his men out across the whole country to record the extent and value of the lands he had fought to acquire twenty years before. In the section for Yorkshire there is an entry for the Manor of 'Hedingeleia'. It is just a one-liner, but the very abbreviated Latin text tells us the extent

The opening words of the Domesday Book entry for Headingley (1086): one line tightly written into the bottom of the page which lists the lands of Ilbert de Lacy in the Skyrack Wapentake in the West Riding of Yorkshire. *(Thoresby Society)*

of taxable land, how much was arable, that there had previously been two manors there under two lords, that there were two 'villeins'(bondsmen) and one plough, and that the manor had previously been worth 40 shillings and now was worth 4 shillings.[1]

The entry for Headingley appears in the pages listing the lands of Ilbert de Laci in the West Riding of Yorkshire.[2] It is shown within the wapentake (an administrative area) called 'Siraches', later and more commonly spelt 'Skyrack'. The name Skyrack is generally believed to mean Shire Oak, the tree marking the place where the shire meetings or court were held. Popular tradition has it that the ancient oak tree which used to stand in Headingley village, close to the Original Oak inn, was the tree which had given its name to the whole of the large Skyrack wapentake, with Headingley as its focal point.

The Norman baron who held Headingley as part of his vast estates, Ilbert de Laci (Lacy) had come over to England from Normandy with William.[3] He came from

---

1. *The Domesday Book and Yorkshire*, University of Hull, 1986. The drop in value, common throughout the county, reflects the devastation caused by William's armies in their battles to subdue the rebellious North.

2. Riding is the Old English word for a third, the county of Yorkshire being divided into three parts, the East, North and West Ridings. For more information on the term 'wapentake' see p.30.

3. W.E.Wightman, 'The Yorkshire Lacys 1066–1193', in *University of Leeds Review*, Vol.X No.2, p.120 (1966).

Lassay, south of Bayeux, hence his name. As part of a strategy to control the North, the King made him overlord of an extensive and powerful new estate, an 'Honour', based at Pontefract, where Ilbert set about building a castle from which he could dominate the surrounding countryside and the important routes which passed through it. This was one of the largest estates in the kingdom and under Ilbert it was divided among a number of other barons who held their lands from him. The manor of Headingley was granted to Walter Poitevin (various spellings of the name exist) from Poitou, who had accompanied William in his strike across the Channel. The former division of the area into two manors, recorded in Domesday, lingered on into later centuries, when a distinction was often made between West Headingley and East Headingley, the latter being the seat of the manor and the location of the village.

Kirkstall Abbey

By the next century Ilbert's grandson, Henry de Lacy, had become overlord of the Honour and William Poitevin was Lord of the Manor of Headingley. It is Henry de Lacy who is credited with the foundation of Kirkstall Abbey.[4] In 1147, in gratitude for his recovery from an illness, he had given the abbot of Fountains Abbey some land at Barnoldswick to found a new abbey, but the project had collapsed; the monks sent there found the climate and the local people inhospitable, and the search began for a new site. The story goes that their abbot, Alexander, stumbled by accident upon what seemed the ideal place, the green and sheltered valley of Kirkstall next to the river, within the manor of Headingley. Henry de Lacy was asked to use

---

4. For an overall survey of the history of Kirkstall Abbey up to dissolution, see Guy Barnes, 'Kirkstall Abbey, 1147–1539: an Historical Study', *PThS* LVIII (1984). The Thoresby Society has also published transcriptions of original documents relating to the Abbey, notably 'The Coucher Book of the Cistercian Abbey of Kirkstall', which contains records of charters relating to the Abbey's property (in Latin), *PThS* VIII (1904).

Kirkstall Abbey from an engraving dated 1769, when the tower was still standing. The manor of Headingley-cum-Burley was granted to Kirkstall Abbey in 1324, following a number of earlier gifts of land there including the site of the Abbey itself. The manor was governed by the Abbey for over 200 years until dissolution in 1539, when all the land reverted to the Crown. *(Thoresby Society)*

his influence to persuade William Poitevin to grant the necessary land.[5] This he duly did, and the new abbey at Kirkstall was founded in 1152. Henry de Lacy is said to have laid the foundations of the great church 'with his own hand', and he gave money to fund the building. By 1182 the Abbey was established, and over the following centuries it flourished, benefiting from numerous endowments and grants of land in many of the townships around Leeds and further afield.

Within its immediate neighbourhood too, the Abbey slowly acquired increasing property. As well as his initial grant of the Abbey site, William Poitevin gave more land in Headingley where farms (granges) were established to

5. A medieval account of the foundation of the Abbey exists, based on earlier sources. See E.K.Kitson Clark, ed., 'Fundacio – The Foundation of Kirkstall Abbey', *PThS* IV (1895).

Engraved by   PUBLISHED BY JOSEPH JOHNSON.   H Le Petit.

South East View of Kirkstall Abbey in 1769.

help support the Abbey (Bar Grange, New Grange and Moor Grange),[6] and his son Thomas and other members of the family made further gifts of land. Then, early in the fourteenth century, the manor passed from the Poitevins to John of Calverley, connected to the Poitevins by marriage. In 1324 John granted the entire manor to the Abbey, with all its dues and revenues. This important gift was the cause of a series of bitter lawsuits brought by Alexander Poitevin, disputing the gift and making accusations of forgery and false witness, but judgement was finally made in favour of the Abbey.[7] So the Abbey took control of Headingley and held the manor for the next 200 years, renting much of the land out to tenant farmers. The early records show that by this time a mill had been established there called Headingley Mill, in the field called 'Bentlay', next to Meanwood Beck but on the Allerton side. There are references too to a Hall, gardens, granges, named fields, and woods: 'Le Meenewude', 'Riggeclyf', and the 'Wetwude', names still familiar today. It is clear that much of the land was enclosed and cultivated or used for grazing, but there was common land too, in particular the Moor, the 'mora de Heddinglay', where local people would have been able to graze their animals, cut peat, dig stone, and collect firewood. The name 'Monk Bridge' is a reminder of the monks' tenure here: a track across the Moor led to this bridge, built across Meanwood Beck around 1300 to provide access to Abbey lands in Allerton.

DISSOLUTION

In 1535 two Commissioners, Richard Layton and Thomas Legh, were despatched by Thomas Cromwell, Henry VIII's minister, to visit the monasteries of northern England

The present Monk Bridge across Meanwood Beck, the name a reminder of the bridge built here by the monks of Kirkstall Abbey around 1300 to provide access to the Abbey's newly-acquired manor of Allerton.

---

6. 'Coucher Book', op.cit., Charters LXVII, LXXIV, LXXV/ VI/ VII/ VIII, and LXXX.

7. 'Coucher Book', op.cit., Charters CCCXCVI/ VII/ VIII; also 'Calverley Charters', *PThS* VI (1904) Charters 170, 184, 212, 213 and 214.

and report on their condition and wealth. It was the first step in the process of dissolution. They arrived at Kirkstall early in 1536 to conduct their survey and valuation. The abbot of Kirkstall was involved in the subsequent uprising known as the Pilgrimage of Grace, but the rebellion was ruthlessly crushed – unlike some others, he escaped execution. In November 1539 Richard Layton returned, and the abbot and 31 members of the Kirkstall community surrendered the Abbey to the Crown.[8] Its roof was stripped of lead, its bells melted down, its walls left to crumble. Its widespread lands were seized and then sold or handed out to those to whom favours were owed in return for services to the King.

In 1543 the site of the Abbey and its 'demesne', the land directly under its control, were granted to Thomas Cranmer, Archbishop of Canterbury, who had supported Henry VIII's case for divorce, had promoted the dissolution of the monasteries, and was a leading figure in the Reformation. The grant was confirmed in Henry's will but when Cranmer was attainted for treason by Queen Mary in 1557 and finally burnt at the stake,[9] his land was repossessed by the Crown. In another reversal of fortune, Cranmer's son Thomas regained it when Elizabeth I came to the throne, but his tenure was only brief. In 1564 a large tract of the Abbey's former lands, comprising Headingley, Burley, Bar Grange, Moor Grange, Armley and adjoining areas, was granted to Robert Savile. At the dissolution this land had produced almost a third of the Abbey's income, so it was a profitable acquisition. In 1583 the Abbey itself, with part of its adjoining demesne lands, was added to this large and valuable estate. There were other smaller grants of the former lands of the Abbey, the most significant in Headingley being the New Grange estate, which came into

---

8. The abbot and monks were granted pensions and some remained in the locality; see Allister Lonsdale, 'The Last Monks of Kirkstall Abbey', *PThS* LIII (Pt III, 1973).

9. He was designated a Protestant martyr, his story told in his contemporary John Foxe's *Book of Martyrs*.

the possession of the Foxcroft family from Halifax; it was later purchased by Anthony Wade, also from Halifax, who had married Judith Foxcroft, and it remained in the Wade family, prominent merchants in Leeds, until bought by the banker William Beckett in 1834. The Beckett family continued to live there until 1910, when the estate was sold to the Corporation for the erection of the city's first teacher training college. It is now the Beckett Park campus of Leeds Metropolitan University.[10]

THE SAVILES OF HOWLEY

Sir Robert Savile,[11] who in 1564 acquired this great swathe of Abbey land, was the illegitimate son of Sir Henry Savile of Thornhill[12] by Margaret Barkston, one of his wife's waiting maids. Robert was not disadvantaged by his illegitimacy; he was his father's favourite and Sir Henry gave him his name and ensured that a part of his estate was made over to him to provide for his future. Sir Robert was said to be a man of outstanding natural ability who achieved great success. He extended his estates, adding substantial possessions around Howley, near Batley and Morley, to the former Abbey lands. It was at Howley that he began the construction of a vast, magnificent mansion, Howley Hall, meant to be the seat for future generations of his family. He died in 1585 and was succeeded by his son, Sir John Savile, aged then about 30, who completed the erection of this great house, said to have cost over £100,000 to build and the object of much admiration.

The coat of arms of the Saviles of Howley. Sir John Savile (1555–1630), politician and courtier, was Lord of the Manor of Headingley. In recognition of his support for the West Riding cloth trade and his help in gaining a Charter from King Charles in 1626, the merchants of Leeds elected him as first Alderman of Leeds and borrowed two owls from his coat of arms for the Corporation's new crest.

---

10. For the history of New Grange/Beckett Park see J. Sprittles, 'New Grange, Kirkstall: its owners and occupants', *PThS* XLVI (1963); and L.Beckett, ed., *City of Leeds Training College – Continuity and Change 1907–2007*, Leeds, 2007.

11. For information on the Saviles of Howley, see Michael Sheard, *Records of the Parish of Batley*, Worksop, 1894; William Smith, ed., *Old Yorkshire*, London, 1881, Vol.I; Norrison Scatchard, *The History of Morley*, Leeds, 1830.

12. Sir Henry Savile was High Sheriff of Yorkshire 1537–41, and a loyal supporter of Henry VIII: J.W.Clay, 'The Savile Family', in *Yorkshire Archaeological Journal*, XXV (1920).

Sir John was a powerful and ambitious man, active at court and in public life, and a significant figure in Leeds history. He held office as Keeper of the Rolls and High Steward of the Barony of Pontefract, he was a Privy Counsellor, and six times MP for the county. His career at court was overshadowed by a bitter feud with the Earl of Strafford (Thomas Wentworth, from another powerful Yorkshire family), and he lost office after complaints of his arrogance and abuse of power, but he survived his fall from favour and was created a Baron in 1628. He took on the role of advocate for the West Riding and the cloth trade and in 1626 supported the cloth merchants in Leeds in their petition to Charles I for a charter incorporating Leeds as a free borough, with significant powers of self-government. He was nominated as the first Alderman of the Borough, an honorary position. In recognition of his powerful support the 1626 Leeds coat of arms incorporated two owls from his family crest, still a familiar emblem of the city today.

Headingley was of course only a part of the large estate which Sir John possessed, but a significant and profitable

Howley Hall. This grandiose house was begun by Sir Robert Savile, who acquired much of the former Abbey land after dissolution including the manor of Headingley and the Abbey itself. The Hall was completed by his son Sir John Savile around 1590. When the Savile estates passed to the Brudenell family in 1671, the house fell into disuse, and in 1717 was blown up and destroyed.

part, particularly after the establishment of Kirkstall Forge around 1617.[13] Sir John had an important role as Lord of the Manor, and it was he who in 1619 granted part of the common land on Headingley village green as the site for a chapel to serve the local residents and commissioned the building work, though it was one of his wealthy local tenants who provided much of the money.

Sir John died in 1630 and was succeeded by his third son, Thomas, his other sons having died early without issue. Thomas was also active in court life: he was Gentleman of the Bedchamber and Treasurer of the Household to Charles I and was created Earl of Sussex in 1644. However, in this tempestuous period of the Civil War, he acquired a reputation as untrustworthy and was accused of forgery and acts of violence, including an abortive attempt to take control of Kirkstall Forge. He was charged with bribery and disloyalty to the King and was briefly imprisoned in the Tower. His estates were sequestered, and he had to buy them back, leaving him deeply in debt. In 1652, probably in an effort to raise money, he granted a long lease for 500 years of a large area of Headingley, around Kirkstall and along the river, initially to Abraham Hinchcliffe, then to John Moore, the curate at Headingley, from whom it descended by marriage to the Graham family.[14] This land was destined to prove very valuable, as the river provided power for the many mills established there in the following centuries, growing ever more

The great seal of Leeds Corporation, 1626, with the two owls from the Savile coat of arms, together with a fleece representing the all-important wool trade.

---

13. For more information on the establishment of the Forge and on Sir John's relationship with his important tenants in Headingley, see J.L.Cruickshank, *Headingley-cum-Burley c1540 to c1784*, PhD Thesis (unpublished), University of Leeds, 2003.

14. A note on the lease is included in the 1793/94 Cardigan Estate Rental: WYAS Leeds, WYL160/220/43. By the 1790s Sir James Graham (1753–1825) was the lessee; he spent a considerable sum of money expanding and modernising the Kirkstall mills.
A prominent lawyer and MP, he was created first Baronet of Kirkstall in 1808; in 1825 he was succeeded by his son Sir Sandford Graham (1788–1852), and then by his grandson, also Sir Sandford (1821–75). Although they took their title from Kirkstall, they never lived there. W.H.MacKean, *The Grahams of Kirkstall*, 1960.

profitable as industrial development gathered pace. The sphere of influence of the Grahams is still visible today in the crowded streets of close-packed terraces built in the nineteenth century to house the workers from the nearby mills: the developers and builders were allowed a free hand.

Thomas Savile remained an unpopular figure, though there are conflicting versions of his story. When he died in 1658, his estates passed to his son James, the second Earl of Sussex, who seems to have taken no part in public life. He died in 1671 aged only 24, just after the death of his one small son and heir. So this family which had risen so rapidly in wealth and power sank in reputation and social position, and the male line died out. On James's death, the Savile estates were inherited by his sister Frances who three years before, in 1668, had married Lord Francis Brudenell, eldest son of the second Earl of Cardigan. She had been given a £5,000 dowry, but on her brother's death she became heiress to a significant estate which now passed into the possession of the Brudenell family. This Yorkshire estate, especially the areas around Howley and Wakefield which were to prove rich in coal, eventually brought the family great wealth.

A Curse?

The fate of Robert Savile's family, extinct within three generations, gave weight to the belief that a curse hung over those who had misappropriated the lands of the Abbey from their original religious purpose: they would meet with misfortune or violent death, and their name would die out. Sir John Savile had had four sons who died in his lifetime without issue; his grandson, James, also died without an heir. The great mansion at Howley, erected at such enormous cost, was destined to be abandoned and then totally destroyed. The later story of the Brudenells, whose last direct heir to the title died childless in 1868, was quoted in support of this tale.[15]

The Brudenells, Earls of Cardigan [16]

After their inheritance, Lord Francis Brudenell and his wife lived occasionally at Howley but mostly in London, enjoying the fashionable life; they were both to die comparatively young, Lady Frances in 1695, and Lord Brudenell in 1698. Their son George inherited the title of Earl of Cardigan from his uncle in 1703, becoming the third Earl at the age of seventeen, and he went then to live at Deene, the ancestral home of the Brudenells in Northamptonshire. Howley Hall, no longer needed, was divided into tenements and let out until 1717 when, apparently on the order of Lord Cardigan, it was destroyed by explosives, blown to pieces. It was said that the local Cardigan agent had persuaded Lord Cardigan of the need to destroy the Hall as it was no longer required and was too expensive to maintain. Local people were shocked and horrified; a poem was written recording how 'this noble mansion met its doom'.[17]

In 1673, two years after the Brudenells acquired the Savile estates, they sold off a substantial portion of their land in Headingley, some 200 acres on the eastern side between the chapel (St Michael's) and the border of the township along Woodhouse Moor, on both sides of Headingley Lane (the area known as Headingley Hill). The purchaser was John Walker from Gawthorpe, who was building up an extensive estate for himself in Headingley. In 1693 he transferred the property, which included farms and houses and the right to a pew in

---

15. Michael Sheard, *Records of the Parish of Batley*, Worksop, 1894, p.140/1.

16. A comprehensive account of the Brudenell family is to be found in: Joan Wake, *The Brudenells of Deene*, London, 1953.

17. *History of the Far-Famed Howley Hall, Batley*, pamphlet published by Fearnsides & Sons, Batley: mainly based on N. Scatchard's *History of Morley*, op.cit. Materials from the ruined Hall were used in nearby buildings. While the Hall has gone, the name still lingers on, attached now to the golf course which occupies the former park.

The South PROSPECT of DEENE HALL.

Deene Park, Northamptonshire (from an old print). From 1514, Deene was the family home of the Brudenells, Earls of Cardigan. The house and park are still in the ownership of the Brudenell family.

Headingley chapel, to his son John Walker (Junior), a wealthy London lawyer who in 1711 was appointed Recorder for Leeds;[18] in addition, this John Walker rented Headingley Hall and the fields near the Ridge from Lord Cardigan. After his death the estate passed to his nephew, another John Walker, and from him to his sister, Mary Bainbrigge. When she died in 1805, the estate was split up between her various descendants who, from the 1820s onwards, began selling the land off in large building plots, leading to the residential development of Headingley Hill with its grand villas and large gardens.

In 1711, not long after the new Earl of Cardigan had taken over the extensive family estates, a survey was commissioned of some of the Yorkshire manors which had

18. Ralph Thoresby, the historian of Leeds, dedicated his famous history *Ducatus Leodiensis* to him (1715). Thoresby was John Walker's cousin and was present at Court when he was appointed Recorder, in place of the candidate favoured by the Corporation. (D.H.Atkinson, *Ralph Thoresby, the Topographer*, Leeds, 1885, Vol. 2).

been inherited from the Saviles. In addition to Headingley cum Burley, the estate included the manors of Bramley, Gildersome, East and West Ardsley and Woodkirk, and land at Howley, New Park, Wakefield, Horsforth, Farnley, and Drighlington. Joseph Dickinson undertook the survey of Headingley among others, and his work provides us with the first maps of the manor and township (p.4). The maps provide field names and a key which gives the names of the tenants and in one version the acreage they rent. The survey book which originally accompanied the maps has unfortunately been lost, but the maps give us a valuable snapshot of the township in 1711, though only of the Cardigan possessions; the Wade and Walker lands and other small freeholdings are left blank.

ESTATE MANAGEMENT [19]

The Earls of Cardigan, based as they were at Deene and with extensive estates nearby in Northamptonshire and Leicestershire, could not administer their valuable Yorkshire estate directly: their head steward employed a locally-based land agent, usually together with a bailiff and woodsman. During the eighteenth century the attitude towards the administration of the estate seems to have been fairly relaxed and there is not much sign of intervention either with the agent or the tenants, though the head steward certainly visited periodically. This easy-going approach is borne out by Elizabeth Beecroft of Kirkstall Forge, in her spirited account of how her family, without any relevant experience, boldly took on the lease of the Forge in 1778; she comments that the tenancy would be 'under Lord Cardegan and they reckon they who gets under him it is as good as half there own'; he was

19. A substantial collection of records relating to the administration of the Cardigan estate in Yorkshire is held by the West Yorkshire Archive Service Leeds in the series WYL160/220.

'a right good landlord'.[20] During this time many cottage encroachments were allowed on the common land and a number of year-to-year tenancies were agreed at low rents. The local estate records were fairly brief and casual.

However, there was a sharp change in the 1790s after the death of the fourth Earl of Cardigan[21] and the succession of his brother James, the fifth Earl. This was a time of exciting and potentially profitable developments on the Yorkshire estate: the value of the many coal deposits was being recognised, new leases were granted for collieries and fresh borings for coal undertaken. A full survey of the estate was commissioned in the period 1792–1798.[22] Instructions were issued to the Yorkshire steward to present his rental accounts in a new, more detailed format and ensure that proper leases were granted and old ones renegotiated.[23] From then on a tougher attitude prevailed and the Yorkshire agent was closely supervised by the Earl's London lawyer, who visited regularly and checked all the accounts rigorously. Headingley became the focus of the Yorkshire estate management when in 1832 the local Cardigan agent, George Hayward (brother of the head steward), came to live in Headingley Hall.

While the Cardigans were absentee landlords, they had an important role as Lord of the Manor. Lord Cardigan's consent had to be obtained for any proposed appropriation of the common land in Headingley, either on the Moor

---

20. Her lively account of the family taking on the Forge is included in A.E., B.F., and H.M.Butler, ed., *The Diary of Thomas Butler of Kirkstall Forge, Yorkshire, 1796–1799*, London, 1906; see also Rodney Butler, *The History of Kirkstall Forge through Seven Centuries 1200–1954*, Leeds, 1954.

21. He had been created first Duke of Montague in 1766, and used that title thereafter. However, as he had no direct heir the title lapsed on his death.

22. *Particulars and Valuation of the Estate of the Rt. Hon. James Earl of Cardigan in the County of York, Surveyed and valued by Jno. Bainbridge, 1792–1798*, NRO Brudenell papers, ASR559. Microfilm in Leeds Local Studies Library, MIC333.323C179.

23. Cardigan Rental, 1793–4. WYAS Leeds, WYL160/220/43.

or on the 'green' or waste land in the village, though the other freeholders had to agree too. Around 1770 an area of nearly 50 acres on the Moor, almost a third, was granted to the curate of Headingley to augment the living; and in 1783 land on the village green was granted for the construction of a charity school. As Lord of the Manor, Lord Cardigan was asked for and usually gave substantial donations for various good causes, and provided some treats for his tenants in the form of annual dinners in the local inn. Some old manorial customs were maintained: the manorial court for Headingley, the Court Baron, continued to meet (it is not clear how regularly) through the eighteenth century and into the nineteenth. The court was summoned by the Cardigan steward or bailiff, with local freeholders as 'jurors', to discuss local issues, often connected with the common land, and to determine penalties – for example, for not fencing the quarry on the Moor to the danger of grazing cattle and passers-by; or not yoking or 'ringing' a pig which wandered and caused general havoc (without a ring in its nose it was difficult to catch).[24] On occasion a new 'pindar' was appointed, to round up loose livestock and put them in the pinfold. Sometimes those present rode or walked round the boundaries of the manor, an ancient method of confirming land boundaries. As the nineteenth century progressed, these old customs died away and it seems unlikely that the Court met after 1832.

The Common Land – Looking for Profit

As Lord of the Manor, Lord Cardigan owned the mineral rights in all the common land, and in 1827 his agents, keen to exploit the booming market for coal, ordered bores to be sunk on Headingley Moor to 'try for coal'.[25] Several bores

---

24. Records of the Court Baron for the Manor of Headingley-cum-Burley, 1716, 1732, 1776–94, 1832. WYAS Leeds, WYL160/220/3, /4, /5, /10.

25. WYAS Leeds, WYL160/220/14, Memoranda, September 1827.

Shaw Lane was originally a track across Headingley Moor leading to Monk Bridge. When the Moor was enclosed in 1834 the road was improved and the land on either side was allocated to various owners and gradually developed. On the right hand side there was a public quarry, the hollow it left still visible today. The name of this part of Monk Bridge Road was changed in the 1860s in honour of John Hope Shaw of Shaw House, a distinguished solicitor and town councillor who was three times Mayor of Leeds. *(Thoresby Society)*

were sunk to a depth of 90 yards but no coal was found – if it had been, the future of the village and the Moor might have been very different. Disappointed, the Cardigan agents looked for another way to wring some profit from the common land, through the well-tried means of enclosure. Nominally the purpose of enclosure was the improvement of 'waste' land for agriculture, but this was not the motive here. There was little open land left in Headingley, just the Moor, depleted by earlier enclosures, and the remnants of the village greens and the road verges; but what there was could prove valuable for future building development, as more people chose to move out of the increasingly uncomfortable atmosphere of the town to live in the outlying villages. So the decision was taken in 1828 to start the long and complex enclosure procedure.[26]

---

26. A detailed study of the Headingley-cum-Burley enclosure will be published by the Thoresby Society in Autumn 2008.

SHAW LANE, HEADINGLEY.   34

THE HEADINGLEY-CUM-BURLEY ENCLOSURE, 1829–1834

In this period a private Act of Parliament was required to authorise the enclosure of common land. Lord Cardigan took the initiative as Lord of the Manor and the major landowner. He still owned more than half the land in the township, some 1500 acres, but he needed the support of the other large landowners with 'rights of common'. They were quick to agree, with the enticing prospect of gaining some free additional land. A petition was submitted to Parliament, a draft Bill agreed, and the enabling Act was passed in 1829.[27] A Commissioner was appointed to carry out the work, but when he died in 1830, the Cardigan agent George Hayward took over, in contravention of the terms of the Act, which excluded interested parties from acting as Commissioners: the other landowners were persuaded to turn a blind eye. It took him four more years to complete the complex procedure of mapping the land, identifying the 'waste', assessing claims from people who already owned property in the township, determining existing and new roads and footpaths, designating public quarries, wells and watering places, and dividing and apportioning the land between the successful claimants. Some plots of common land in Burley and Headingley villages and on the Moor were sold by public auction in 1831 to raise money to cover all the heavy legal costs involved. The Enclosure Award was finally signed and sealed in November 1834, with its accompanying map.[28] As Lord of the Manor and the major landowner Lord Cardigan was allotted over 28 acres, nearly half the available land, and 22 other owners got a share, though many of the allotments were very small. So the remnants of the village green in Headingley and the wild open Moor became private property, fenced off, the old footpaths blocked, and the common land barred from use by the local villagers. There were signs of protest, with stakes and fences repeatedly pulled up, but the process was inexorable. The village plots were quickly built on, those on the Moor more gradually. Even now the shape of the plots is still sometimes discernible and some of the large gardens around Moor Road and Claremont Road retain a memory of the green spaces of the old Moor.

---

27. 10 Geo.IV cap.17

28. WYAS Leeds, RDP39/162: bound copy of the Award and Map. An earlier version of the map and associated terrier (schedule of lands) from 1831 and a numerical survey of 1829 are to be found in WYL160/35, but these show significant differences from the final 1834 version.

James Thomas Brudenell, 7th Earl of Cardigan (1797−1868). In 1837 he inherited the title and the extensive family estates, including the manor of Headingley and about half the land in the township. His life and military career were marked by scandal and controversy. He is remembered particularly for his leadership of the notorious charge of the Light Brigade at Balaclava in the Crimea in September 1854 − and for the woollen coat which he wore to ward off the chills of the Crimean winter, giving his name to what became an iconic British winter garment.

The Seventh Earl

In 1837 Robert, the sixth Earl of Cardigan, died and his only son, James Thomas Brudenell, became the seventh Earl.[29] He inherited the vast family estates and an income estimated at £40,000 a year, which nevertheless proved inadequate for his extravagant needs and way of life. Already notorious for well-publicised scandals both in his private life and in his military career, he was to continue to lead a life marked by dispute and controversy. He fought two duels (forbidden by law); was arrested and tried in the House of Lords for murder but exonerated on a technicality; was embroiled in a series of bitter conflicts

29. There are several very readable books about the seventh Earl and his role in the Crimea: Cecil Woodham-Smith, *The Reason Why*, 1953; Donald Thomas, *Cardigan, the Hero of Balaclava*, 1974; and Saul David, *The Homicidal Earl: The Life of Lord Cardigan*, 1997.

with his officers which resulted in a public reprimand and suspension; and in his private life engaged in a series of sexual adventures which provided sensational fodder for the newspapers.

Almost as soon as he took over the family estates in 1837, there was a change of direction in their management in order to raise some ready money. Some of the property in Yorkshire was mortgaged to release cash, and in 1841 John Hayward, his head steward, wrote to his brother George, the Yorkshire agent, that the mortgages were 'making sad havoc' of the estate and would 'ultimately produce serious mischief'.[30] In 1850 a decision was taken to sell off the land on the Moor allotted to Lord Cardigan in the enclosure, together with some fields close to the village which it was hoped would easily find buyers. The land was put up for sale by auction in 1850 but only a few plots sold. In 1851 fresh plans were drawn up by George Hayward, dividing the land into smaller plots and delineating new streets to facilitate building development, in the hope of attracting small developers and speculative builders (p.184). Further auctions were held in 1851 and 1852, sales trickled on over the following years, and the planned new roads became reality. George Hayward's 1851 plan was to determine the way in which the village developed, both in its road layout and in the piecemeal building which took place, its impact still visible today. We owe Chapel Street, Chapel Place, Bennett Road, Alma Road, Grove Road, and Claremont Road to this plan.[31]

In 1854 came news of what was to prove Lord Cardigan's most famous and controversial exploit, which transformed him from public villain to acclaimed hero. At the battle of Balaclava in the Crimea he led the desperate charge of the Light Brigade against the Russian guns.

---

30. Letter from John Hayward to George Hayward, 19.4.1841. WYAS Leeds, WYL160/220/23.

31. For more information on the sales and on the development of the Claremont Road area, see E.J.Bradford, *A Respectable Terrace – the story of Woodbine Terrace, Headingley*, Leeds, 2000.

A military disaster in terms of bungled communication and the appalling loss of more than two thirds of the men and their horses, the charge was translated in the public mind into an emblem of courage and fortitude in the face of overwhelming odds, immortalised for later generations in Tennyson's famous poem. When Lord Cardigan returned to England, it was to the triumphal music of 'See the Conquering Hero Comes'; he was invited to Windsor to tell Queen Victoria and Prince Albert the full story; he was cheered and feted wherever he went and women wept when they heard him speak. In Leeds in 1856 a great dinner was held in his honour and he was presented with a costly ceremonial sword and an illuminated address from the people of Yorkshire. When he responded he was visibly moved and was warmly cheered, but the *Times* was to dismiss his Leeds speech as a falsification of history, and doubts and accusations gathered round him, although he won a case for libel against one of his main critics. His role in the famous charge remains today a topic for debate, but there seems little doubt that the adulation he received went to his head and fostered his vanity and arrogance.

In 1857, aged 60, Lord Cardigan began a passionate affair with the beautiful and talented Adeline Horsey de Horsey, the 32-year-old daughter of his friend Admiral de Horsey. She openly became his mistress, to public disapproval and scandal. In 1858, on the death of his estranged wife, they married, but Adeline was still not accepted socially; Queen Victoria refused to receive her and she was excluded from public life.[32] There were no children from the marriage. Their life was focussed on Deene, where enormous sums of money were spent on grandiose schemes of improvement, and they spent their time indulging in the expensive pleasures of hunting and yachting at Cowes. For many years Lord Cardigan had found it difficult to live within his income and now

---

32. In 1909 she took revenge by publishing her scandalous and racy memoirs, *My Recollections*, which caused a rumpus when they appeared and provoked the displeasure of the Royal Family.

he plunged further and further into debt, repeatedly mortgaging his estates, with a patrician disregard for the future and with no heir to provide for. In March 1868, he died quite suddenly after a fall from his horse. His funeral was as solemn and magnificent as he could have wished, a funeral for a hero. His courage, generosity and gallantry were remembered, his failings forgotten.

Adeline remained at Deene, on the fringes of society, her conduct becoming increasingly eccentric and scandalous. After unsuccessfully pursuing Benjamin Disraeli in the hope of marriage, she suddenly, in 1873, married a Portuguese Count whom she had met in Paris, the Count of Lancastre.[33] On their honeymoon they toured the Yorkshire estate and on 18 September visited Kirkstall Abbey and the Forge, where she arrived, dressed in 'blue

The banquet held in Leeds in the hall of the Stock Exchange, Albion Street, on 30 August 1856 in honour of Lord Cardigan, the hero of Balaclava. A ceremonial sword costing 250 guineas was presented to him, on its handle an enamelled portrait of 'his lordship dashing forward in the attack upon the Russian guns'. While the banquet was for men only, the picture shows a cluster of women gazing at the hero from the sidelines. *(Leeds Library)*

---

33. He claimed descent from John of Gaunt, Duke of Lancaster, a claim many viewed as highly dubious. His name is still remembered in two Bramley street names.

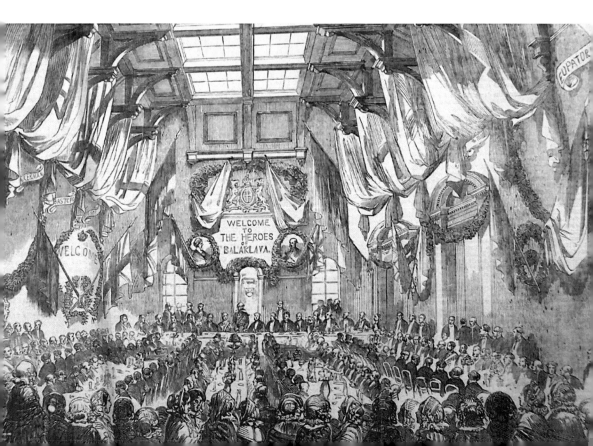

PARTICULARS No. 1.—Lots 1 to 39.

THE CARDIGAN ESTATES, YORKSHIRE—FIRST PORTION.

LEEDS.

Particulars, Plans and Conditions of Sale

OF HIGHLY IMPORTANT

FREEHOLD PROPERTIES

Situate at Headingley, Burley and Far Headingley, in the Township of

HEADINGLEY-CUM-BURLEY,

Forming the most fashionable suburbs of the important Town of Leeds, with easy access thereto from Headingley and Kirkstall Stations, on the North Eastern and Midland Railways, and by Two Tramway routes: comprising

MOST ELIGIBLE BUILDING ESTATES

Judiciously divided into convenient lots to suit the requirements of Builders and others;

NUMEROUS DWELLING HOUSES & COTTAGES

Residential Properties ; The Cardigan Arms, Burley ; The Grove Spinning Mills ; Bridge Oil Mills ; Stone Quarries ;

SEVERAL COMPACT FARMS

AND

DETACHED LANDS,

THE WHOLE COMPRISING AN AREA OF ABOUT

422 ACRES.

Which will be Sold by Auction,

BY MESSRS.

CHINNOCK, GALSWORTHY & CHINNOCK

At the "ALBERT HALL," COOKRIDGE STREET, LEEDS,

On TUESDAY, the 11th day of DECEMBER, 1888,

At Twelve for One o'Clock precisely—IN 43 LOTS.

May be viewed by permission of the Tenants, and Particulars and Conditions of Sale obtained of Messrs. WALKER and MAWSON-WALKER, Solicitors, 12, Furnival's Inn, E.C.; of Messrs. ROOPER & WHATELY, Solicitors, 17, Lincoln's Inn, W.C.; of Messrs. MARTIN & FENWICK, Surveyors, 1, Park Place, Leeds; and of

Messrs. CHINNOCK, GALSWORTHY & CHINNOCK, Land Agents and Surveyors, 11, Waterloo Place, Pall Mall, London, S.W.

F. CARPENTER, Printer, 27, Southampton Buildings, and Westminster.

Particulars of Sale of the first Portion of the Cardigan Estates, 11 December 1888. The lots for sale on this day included many village properties in Headingley. The auction continued over four days, and the property offered for sale included Kirkstall Abbey and Abbey House. (Thoresby Society)

satin with lace flounces and adornments', in a chariot drawn by four horses and outriders, to a salute of fifteen guns. Climbing on a table, she addressed her 'Yorkshire tenantry', while her new husband looked on, bemused. She commented later that he had not known what large estates she possessed and how closely she was in touch with her tenants.[34]

34. The *Yorkshire Post* gave an account of the visit the next day, describing how hundreds of people, 'hard-handed artisans and members of the lower ten thousand, pressed up to the carriage and were allowed to kiss the kid-gloved hand of her ladyship'. Lady Cardigan gave her own glowing account of the visit in *My Recollections*, op.cit., and there is a later record in the leaflet *The Memorable Visit to Kirkstall Abbey and Kirkstall Forge of the Countess of Cardigan 1873* produced by Hugh Myddleton Butler in 1938 (Thoresby Society).

But this rosy picture was far from the truth. In fact, her estates were now being administered by trustees through the Court of Chancery, with power to sell property to repay some of the enormous debts left by Lord Cardigan. Mortgages on the Yorkshire estates alone amounted to some £300,000. From 1869 onwards land in Headingley and elsewhere was offered for sale, but the need to raise money became yet more pressing as the bailiffs moved in at Deene. In December 1888, in a huge four-day auction, almost the whole of the remaining Cardigan estate in Headingley, Kirkstall and Burley, including Kirkstall Abbey itself, went under the hammer, together with Hawksworth Woods and property in Bramley, Drighlington, Gildersome and elsewhere.[35] This enormous sale of some 200 lots attracted a large attendance and realised a substantial amount of money: £35,195 on the first day alone. But many lots, including Kirkstall Abbey and Abbey House, did not reach their reserve and had to be withdrawn.[36] Sales were negotiated in the following months, including, perhaps most significantly for Headingley, Lot 17a, over seventeen acres of 'pasture and woodland, ripe for development' along Cardigan Road, which was bought by 'a company of gentlemen' who had plans to create a magnificent ground for cricket and football in Leeds. They founded an enterprise which remains today a local and national landmark.

So the Cardigan estate in Headingley was finally dismantled, freeing up yet more land for development and leaving echoes only in names, Cardigan Road, the

---

35. Particulars of Sale, Albert Hall, Cookridge Street, Leeds, 11–14 December, 1888; Auctioneers, Messrs. Chinnock, Galsworthy & Chinnock of London (Thoresby Society).

36. Immediately after the auction, Councillor Edmund Wilson, a keen historian and founder in 1889 of the Thoresby Society, made an offer of the reserve for Kirkstall Abbey (£10,000) and Abbey House, in the hope that the Council would find the money for the Abbey and prevent its falling into private hands. In the event the flamboyant entrepreneur Colonel North stepped in, paid the price, and in a magnificent gesture gave the Abbey as a gift to the citizens of Leeds.

Cardigan Arms pub, Cardigan Fields, and so on. Adeline, Lady Cardigan, lost the Yorkshire estate she had so enjoyed visiting. She and the Count of Lancastre stayed together for only six years, and from then on she lived alone at Deene, increasingly isolated and outrageous in behaviour and dress, the subject of numerous whispered stories. She lived to see the outbreak of the First World War but died in 1915, aged 91. Deene passed to another branch of the Brudenell family.

THE SHIRE OAK

A MODEST FADED plaque set into the stone wall on the main road between the Original Oak pub and Shire Oak Road marks the place where once a massive, ancient oak tree stood, 'the principal object in the township of Headingley' according to the nineteenth century guide books, reputed even then to be over a thousand years old, a link with Headingley's far distant past. After centuries of slow decay its skeletal remains finally collapsed in May 1941, and the plaque was set up as a record of this famous Headingley landmark.

There are no medieval records of the tree, but by the eighteenth century it had become the object of much interest and speculation. It was clearly already very old and 'venerable' when Ralph Thoresby, the Leeds antiquary, wrote about it in the early 1700s,[1] and it was thought that it might date back even to Roman times. It certainly aroused Thoresby's interest and he surmised (his opinion supported, he claimed, by 'several learned and ingenious Gentlemen') that this could be the very oak tree which had given its name to the 'Skyrack wapentake', the ancient division of the county in which Headingley lay.

---

1. In his history of Leeds, *Ducatus Leodiensis*, published in 1715.

'The Skyrack Oak, Headingley', a pen and ink sketch dated 1836 by John N. Rhodes (1809–1842). The rough notices nailed to the tree can be read: 'THE ORIGINAL OAK from which the wapentake is named SKYRACK – HEADINGLEY'. *(Thoresby Society)*

He understood the name Skyrack, spelt Siraches in Domesday Book in 1086 and Skire-ake by Thoresby himself, to mean 'Shire Oak', and this has been the most commonly accepted meaning, though more recently it has been interpreted as 'Bright Oak', from the Anglo-Saxon. The wapentake was an administrative area (the term survived into the twentieth century for taxation purposes), and the oak which was its focal point was thought to be the place in Anglo-Saxon times where the local court was held and the clan gathered to take decisions, voting by holding up their weapons, hence the name.[2] There was no hard evidence that the Headingley oak was the original 'Skyrack' and Thoresby's later editor, T. D. Whitaker, thought it unlikely,[3] but there were no other candidates extant, and

2. The word itself is Scandinavian: see David Hey, *Yorkshire from AD 1000*, 1986, p.4.

3. T.D.Whitaker, *Loidis and Elmete*, Vol.I, p.117 (1816).

the tree was indeed exceptionally imposing in its great size and age, so Thoresby's theory became generally accepted and featured in guidebooks and directories. It opened the way for a number of romantic nineteenth century versions of great clan meetings in the middle of Headingley in the shade of the massive oak tree, with the glint of brandished weapons. There was even dark speculation that it had been part of a 'Druidical grove', the location of 'the horrible religious rites of the ancient Britons'.[4]

Local people saw an opportunity to exploit the historical connection and in the very early nineteenth century a rough notice was nailed to the tree, declaring it to be 'The ORIGINAL OAK from which the Wapentake is named SKYRACK', with 'HEADINGLEY' underneath to make sure people knew where they were: an early

A romantic drawing of the Oak in 1854 by the artist Thomas Sutcliffe (1828–1871), who lived at this time in Far Headingley. The artist and his wife and child are depicted at the foot of the tree. The child was Frank Meadow Sutcliffe who, when the family moved to Whitby, gained fame for his photographs of local scenes. The drawing was given to the Thoresby Society by Thomas Sutcliffe's widow in 1902. *(Thoresby Society)*

4. Edward Parsons, op.cit., p.190.

example of opportunist tourist advertising. This aroused a scornful reaction from the sceptical Whitaker: 'The patriarchal plant has lately been condemned to advertise every credulous passenger of what is probably a falsehood…'[5] However, the notice was to remain in place into the 1850s. Both the local public houses called themselves after the tree – the Original Oak and the Skyrack – and it figured in later names too, like Shire Oak Road, Shire Oak Street, and Oak Terrace in Bennett Road. The name still resonates: in 2006, after a poll of parents, 'Shire Oak' was adopted as the name for the new school formed from the merger of St Michael's and Headingley (Bennett Road) Primary Schools.

The tree stood on what was originally common land, at the top end of the old village green, overshadowing the road and the few small cottages straggling along it, on the

An early glass slide (c1852), showing the Oak over-shadowing the main road. Part of the front of the Skyrack Inn can be seen on the left, with a shop and cottages behind. The photograph gives some idea of the significance of the tree in the surrounding landscape, even in extreme old age. *(Thoresby Society)*

5. T.D. Whitaker, op. cit.

A drawing by Walter Braithwaite c1880 of the Oak before it was enclosed in railings, with a side view of the Skyrack pub across the narrow main road and Chantrell's church (demolished 1885) visible beyond. A tree can be seen growing in the road between the church and the pub: this was meant to be a replacement oak, grown from one of the acorns of the original tree. *(Thoresby Society)*

corner of the lane leading up to Headingley Hall, the ancient manor house. Towards the end of the eighteenth century, however, when the tree was already in decay, a cottage was built by its side (where the HSBC bank now stands, at the corner with Shire Oak Road) and a wall was built enclosing the tree within the cottage garden. There it remained until the 1890s when the need to widen the road and the pavement for the installation of overhead wires for the new electric trams meant that the garden wall had to

THE OLD OAK, HEADINGLEY.

A postcard from c1905 showing the Oak enclosed by railings. Its upper branches have gone though it still bears some leaves at low level. The low wall which had previously stood in front of it had to be moved back in 1898/9 to make room for the poles carrying the cables for the electric trams introduced in 1900. On the extreme left the new oak which had been grown in the central enclosure in the road can be seen in full leaf. This had to be dug out in 1921 to make room for the memorial for the Headingley men killed in the 1914–18 War.

be rebuilt further back, leaving the old tree marooned in the middle of the pavement, protected by a low circular wall and iron railings – an ignominious fate according to some. In the new era of the postcard at the turn of the century it was the favourite Headingley subject, viewed from every possible angle but now a rather sad sight, very dilapidated and clearly nearing the end of its long life.

Until the 1900s the tree continued to produce a few leaves and acorns but when a large top branch was blown off in a gale all signs of life ceased and only the hollow trunk remained. This inevitable outcome had been foreseen and efforts had been made to keep the tradition of the Shire Oak alive: one of its acorns had been planted in an enclosure at the road junction between the church and the two pubs, so that a new tree would grow not too far away from the old one. By the turn of the century it was growing strongly and can be seen in pictures of the time.

However in 1921, after the First World War, it was decided that this spot in the heart of what was still thought of as 'the village' was the right and proper place for the erection of a war memorial in memory of Headingley's many dead, and that is where the memorial stands today, honouring the long, sad roll-call of 125 Headingley men who died in the War, 72 of them members of the congregation at the neighbouring St Michael's Church. The decision to uproot the tree which had been planted there to make room for the memorial caused much concern and became the subject of discussion at a meeting of the Thoresby Society, anxious that steps should be taken to preserve the original if this descendant was to be lost – the Oak was not only a Leeds landmark, it was claimed, but 'a whole volume of English history'.[6] In the event an acorn from the tree was planted in the churchyard, a 'grandson' of the ruined original nearby, but unfortunately it failed to grow.

Collapse

Twenty years later, in May 1941, in the midst of another world war, the remains of the old original oak finally collapsed. It was said to be a quiet end – it 'gave a sigh and fell forward on the rails surrounding it'. The Council had discussed trying to prop it up, but had been unable to get hold of the steel required: it was all needed for the war effort. The *Yorkshire Post*, amid news of the desperate battle for Crete and the sinking of HMS Hood and then the Bismarck, still spared space for the loss of this 'link with the remote past of Yorkshire', the tree which had been a landmark for the thousands who used to get off the tram and the bus at that famous Headingley corner, on their way to watch the cricket: 'Headingley is accustomed to collapse. Has not even England collapsed there before now, when the Australian bowling proved too deadly? But a collapse took place yesterday which even the most hardened Headingleyite could not see without a pang...'[7]

---

6. *Yorkshire Post*, 13.5.1921.

7. *Yorkshire Post*, 28.5.1941.

Madonna and Child, carved by Robert Thompson of Kilburn from the wood of the Shire Oak after its collapse in 1941. The figure was auctioned to raise money for the Lord Mayor's Fund for War Charities. It is now in St Michael's Church.

There was much concern to preserve the Shire Oak's memory. It was decided to erect a plaque on the wall nearby as a record of the tree and its ancient history, and what was left of the wood was preserved. The three largest pieces were sent to well-known sculptors, the resulting carvings to be sold in aid of the Lord Mayor's Fund for War Charities. Robert Thompson of Kilburn, the famous 'Mouseman', used the wood to sculpt a small Madonna and Child. This little figure, bought for £25 by an anonymous donor, has happily come home to Headingley and can still be seen today in St Michael's Church. Richard Perry Bedford of the Victoria and Albert Museum carved a head of King Charles, and Major Alan L. Durst of London carved the head of a Bishop's staff, with St George and the Dragon. These pieces were also sold in aid of the Lord Mayor's Fund.[8] Other small pieces of the wood were framed, with a history of the tree, signed by the Mayor, and sold. One of them hangs now on the wall in the Original Oak pub, having been rescued quite recently from oblivion – it was discovered among old files in the pub company headquarters and thought at first to be just an old picture until its significance was realised.

After the war it was decided that a new oak tree should be planted to replace the old landmark and maintain the tradition of so many centuries. In April 1956 an oak sapling was planted close to the site of the old one, on the pavement but rather further back, out of the way of the traffic.[9] It is still there in the corner of the wall, mostly ignored and unrecognised by the numerous passers-by. The lettering of the plaque on the wall, which was white and bright when it was put in place, grows increasingly faint and difficult to read. It is surely time for it to be restored and for the memory of this ancient link with the past to be revived.

---

8. *Yorkshire Post*, 10.11.1941, *Yorkshire Evening Post*, 20.1.1944.

9. *Yorkshire Evening Post*, 6.4.1956; *Yorkshire Post*, 7.4.1956.

The oak tree planted in 1956 as a replacement of the Shire Oak. It continues to flourish in its corner of the pavement but its significance is unmarked, and the nearby plaque recording the old tree is almost illegible.

HEADINGLEY HALL

THE MANOR HOUSE

WHEN YOU TURN the corner from the main road in Headingley into Shire Oak Road and look ahead, you see before you the line of the ancient lane which led up to Headingley's medieval manor house, Headingley Hall. The subsequent bends in the road mark a much later extension of the road created in the 1870s when the fields which had surrounded the Hall were sold off for development. The Hall itself has been rebuilt and altered many times during the centuries: the building we see now dates in part from the late eighteenth century, but with many later alterations.

There has been a manor house on this site for many centuries. There are records of a hall here in the fourteenth century,[1] and it may well have been the manorial centre long before, from Anglo-Saxon times. When the manor was granted to Kirkstall Abbey in 1324, the house was not needed as the residence for the manorial lord and it was leased to tenants, who farmed the surrounding land – a pattern which continued through later centuries. After the dissolution of the Abbey, the manor was one of several

---

1. 'The Coucher Book of the Cistercian Abbey of Kirkstall', op.cit. Charters CCCIV and CCCCXXXIV. An article on the early history of Headingley Hall by Michael Collinson will be published by the Thoresby Society in Autumn 2008.

acquired by Robert Savile and passed on to his son, Sir John Savile, who had no need of the house at Headingley to live in: his family home was the vast and magnificent Hall at Howley, and so Headingley Hall continued to be rented out, together with the surrounding fields.

At this stage it was still a grand residence, attracting distinguished tenants. In the mid seventeenth century, the house was occupied by John Killingbeck, from a prominent and wealthy Leeds merchant family, a leading member of the Corporation, an Alderman, and Mayor of Leeds in 1677. The stone arch to the side of the present house bears a date stone of 1649, with the initials 'JK', which suggests that he may have rebuilt or extended the house in that year. In the same year, on 15 February, his son John was born at the Hall, and he was later baptised in Headingley chapel. This John also played an important role in the town. He was Vicar of Leeds from 1690 until his death in 1716: a greatly esteemed figure in the Church, a benefactor of Leeds Charity School and other good causes, and a close friend of Ralph Thoresby, the antiquarian, who wrote of him with warm affection and admiration. He was said to be so habitually generous that his wife often took money from his pocket at night to put into safekeeping, or it would be given away by the next day! Ralph Thoresby, of course, was familiar with Headingley Hall, the birthplace of his friend, 'a venerable old Fabrick ... near the Skire-ake' (the Shire Oak), he called it.[2]

By 1711, when Joseph Dickinson drew up his map of the Cardigan estate in Headingley, the old Hall had lost status. It was shown as part of a large farm (118 acres), which included all the surrounding fields along the Ridge to Batty Wood and down to Meanwood Beck. The Hall and fields were rented to a farmer, Joshua Dinsdale, as an addition to the neighbouring estate of John Walker, an eminent lawyer who held the important post of Recorder of Leeds from 1711–29. He had acquired the estate from his father, who had bought a large chunk of land extending

2. Ralph Thoresby, *Vicaria Leodiensis*, 1724.

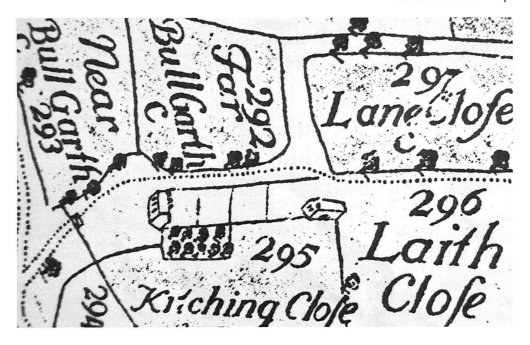

from Woodhouse Moor to the village centre from Lord Cardigan in 1673. It is not clear whether John Walker ever lived in the Hall himself – it seems more probable that he built himself a newer, smarter house elsewhere on his estate (see below) and the Hall became the residence of his tenant who managed the farm on his behalf.

The connection with the Walkers seems to have been broken in the mid eighteenth century, and the Hall and farm were rented off to others. The Hall remained in use as the main residence of the tenant of the farm, which was still the largest on the Cardigan estate in Headingley. From the 1760s up to 1793, the tenant was Jeremiah Nicholson, described in the Chapel register, where the baptism of his son was recorded in 1766, as 'Farmer, of Headingley Hall'. By 1795 he had gone and in a lease dated 13 February 1795[3] the Hall, with its barn, stable, yard, garden and out-buildings, together with the surrounding fields amounting to some 100 acres, was let by the Earl of Cardigan to Samuel Waddington, 'Corn Factor and Farmer'. The lease

Headingley Hall in 1711. This extract from the 1711 Cardigan Estate map shows the Hall with its orchard and kitchen garden and the home farm behind. A lane leads to the Hall from the main road through a gate, then along its side towards the Ridge; this public footpath was closed after the 1834 enclosure and replaced by the newly-formed Wood Lane. The Hall was largely rebuilt in the late eighteenth century and has since undergone numerous alterations and extensions.

---

3. Northamptonshire Record Office, BRUD I.xv.5.

was for 21 years at an annual rent of £100. It included a number of conditions relating to the husbandry of the farm: rotation of crops; fallow periods; and regular manuring of the land ('twelve sufficient cartloads of manure'): the Cardigan estate wanted to ensure the land was well looked after. Batty Wood was specifically excluded: woods were a valuable resource and mainly kept under direct estate control. Poor Samuel Waddington did not enjoy his new lease for long: the *Intelligencer* of 10 August 1795 recorded the death of 'Mr. Samuel Waddington, farmer, of Headingley, of an apoplectic fit, whilst at his dinner'.

REBUILDING

His tenancy was apparently taken over by another member of the family, John Waddington. In 1798, when Jonathan Bainbridge completed his survey and valuation of the Cardigan estate in Yorkshire,[4] he listed John Waddington, Gentleman, as by far the largest tenant in the manor of Headingley, with over 100 acres of land. The property included: 'A Capital Messuage, Barn, Stables and every usefull Outbuilding, Fold, Garden etc. All newly erected'. So it looks as though the Hall was rebuilt or at least extensively altered during the 1790s. John Waddington was an active tenant and the Survey records that he had also built a new cloth mill and reservoir on the land known as the Bentleys,[5] and had improved the land and built additional buildings, spending over £1,500 in the process. He was given a new lease in February 1798 for a period of 21 years, and charged a higher rent.

The Waddingtons continued as tenants into the early nineteenth century but around 1819, according to the Cardigan rent records, the tenancy passed to John Thompson, Samuel Waddington's grandson, who continued to run

4. Northamptonshire Record Office, BRUD ASR559. There is a microfilm copy in Leeds Local Studies Library, MIC 333.323 C179.

5. Later known as Grove Mill – see W.A. Hopwood and F.P.Casperson, *Meanwood*, Leeds, 1986. Now demolished and the site developed for housing.

the farm and live in the Hall. However, he died in 1822 aged only 36, and his mother died in 1829, breaking the tenancy. The Cardigan head steward, John Hayward, took the opportunity to put forward a proposal that his brother George, agent for the Yorkshire estate, should take over the tenancy of the house, stables and garden and around six acres of land, so separating the house from the rest of the farm. The house was to be improved and updated to the tune of some £200;[6] a water closet was to be installed (a luxury at the time), a new pantry provided, a decorative archway created in the entrance hall, and so on. Lord Cardigan agreed and George Hayward moved into the Hall at an annual rent of £35, later increased to £50 when, as so often happens, the cost of the work exceeded the estimate. In the same year, 1832, he married, probably the reason for his move into this large and prestigious house.[7]

THE OLD FARM

Now the connection of the Hall with its home farm was broken. The fields were let off separately to another tenant called Thompson (presumably a member of the same family), together with the barn and outbuildings and a cottage to live in. The farm continued as a working farm until the 1870s, when the Cardigan estate sold off its fields for building development, leaving the farm buildings behind, still with a barn, stable and cowhouse as well as the cottage. The property, called then 'The Old Farm', was bought by George Corson, the architect responsible for

---

6. WYAS Leeds, WYL160/220/16.

7. He married Eleanora Whitaker (1798–1845), daughter of Jonas Whitaker of Greenholme, Burley-in-Wharfedale, the wealthy owner of Greenholme Mill. Built in 1792, this was one of the largest textile mills in the area, originally employing many pauper children brought up from London. Another Whitaker daughter married William Fison, who in partnership with W.E. Forster, the distinguished statesman responsible for the 1870 Education Act, bought the Mill and the associated estate in 1848. In 1871 the Mill employed over 1,000 hands. The building still stands, out of sight next to the river.

much of the development of Shire Oak Road. By the time it came up for sale again in 1901, it had been transformed into a large private residence.[8] This range of buildings, certainly in existence in the late eighteenth century and detailed in the 1798 survey, has survived into the present and is still in use, though for purposes very different from its agricultural origins. It now houses the Yorkshire College of Music and Drama, Shire Oak Road.[9]

The 'Old Farm', now the Yorkshire College of Music and Drama in Shire Oak Road. This eighteenth century building was once the farm attached to Headingley Hall. It was separated from the Hall in 1832 but continued as a working farm until the Cardigan estate sold off its fields for building development in the 1870s, when Shire Oak Road and Street were planned.

8. Sale Particulars: Dunearn and the Old Farm, 18.7.1901 (Thoresby Society).

9. During the Second World War it became the home of Madame Lilian Stiles-Allen, a well-known concert soprano, who took students there for singing lessons, among them Julie Andrews, who found the old house eerie (Richard Stirling, *Julie Andrews*, Portrait, 2007). Mme.Stiles-Allen generously gave the house to the Yorkshire College of Music and Drama in 1968 as their new home.

The Haywards

George Hayward, the tenant of the Hall from 1832, was an influential figure in Headingley and played a significant part in its development between 1830 and 1854, when he died suddenly on a visit to London.[10] He had his own practice as a surveyor, with an office in Albion Street for a time, but his main job was as agent to Lord Cardigan, the principal landowner in Headingley and Lord of the Manor.[11] As such he was closely involved in all matters relating to his property and tenants, and was responsible for the organisation of the early land sales as the estate began to be dismantled, and for formulating plans for new development in and around the village. He had a finger in a number of pies: he took over the role of commissioner for the Headingley-cum-Burley enclosure when the previous commissioner died; he was involved with work on the commutation of tithes; he was the surveyor for the major re-routing of the Leeds-Otley Turnpike Road in 1840; he played a part in the establishment of the new Methodist chapel; and he was a trustee and Honorary Secretary of the Town School. He was also for a time a member of the Leeds Town Council, on the Watch Committee, so was active on a wider stage too. He was reputedly a fiery, argumentative figure, not averse to dispute and conflict. However, he was not a well-known public figure in Leeds and his name is mostly forgotten, in spite of the influence he had on local developments. In contrast, his eldest son, also George Hayward, was to achieve some national fame.

10. Aged 60. He is buried at Otley Parish Church, with his wife and three of their children. After his death, all his working papers seem to have been gathered together and deposited with his solicitors and then with the West Yorkshire Archive Service, Leeds: reference WYL160/220. Their survival was fortunate, as they provide a detailed insight into the administration of the Cardigan estate in Yorkshire in the nineteenth century.

11. He had a much wider remit than just Headingley, as he was responsible for the administration of the whole of Lord Cardigan's Yorkshire estate.

'HE FELL AMONG THIEVES'

An exotic and tragic story[12] is linked with the Haywards and Headingley Hall. George Hayward and his wife Eleanora had six children, but only three survived childhood. Their eldest remaining son, George Jonas Whitaker Hayward, was born at the Hall in 1839. He was sent away to school after his mother's early death, but had to leave when he was only 15 as his father had also died suddenly. At 20, in search of adventure and action, he joined the army, with help from Lord Cardigan who purchased his commission for him. He was sent to India where he developed a passionate interest in the people, languages and geography of the Northwest frontier, but army life failed to provide the excitement he craved. In 1868 he resigned his commission and offered himself to the Royal Geographical Society (RGS) to explore and map these remote, dangerous and still unknown frontier regions. At the same time he was given undercover orders to report on the military and political situation in this isolated, difficult territory: he was both explorer and spy. He travelled sometimes in disguise, and endured danger, captivity and extreme hardship, with a reckless disregard for his own safety. The information he fed back to the RGS won him its coveted Gold Medal. But finally, in 1870, after becoming embroiled in tribal intrigue and conflict, he was murdered at Darkot, in what is now the Northern Areas of Kashmir. He was buried at Gilgit, where the headstone bearing his epitaph can still be seen. The romantically tragic tale of his execution at dawn, after his final request to watch the sun rise one last time, inspired Henry Newbolt to write an emotional commemorative poem, *He Fell among Thieves*, which became a favourite in its day, with its sentimental and patriotic overtones.[13]

George Jonas Whitaker Hayward the explorer, shown in this extraordinary early photograph in native dress surrounded by trophies and weapons. He was born at Headingley Hall in 1839, and after school and a period in the army in India, undertook the dangerous task of exploring and mapping the remote northern reaches of Kashmir. He was murdered there in 1870, aged only 31. *(Reproduced with the permission of the Royal Geographical Society)*

LATER TENANTS

After George Hayward's death in 1854, the Hall was again offered for rent by the Cardigan estate. The first tenant was John Kendall, head of the firm of Kendall & Co., upholsterers and cabinet makers, of West Bar and Basinghall Street.[14] By 1872 a new tenant had moved in, Samuel Ingham, a timber merchant, partner in the large timber and furniture firm of Illingworth, Ingham & Co. In 1884, when the Cardigan estate had already sold much of the surrounding land and Shire Oak Road was being constructed, he purchased the Hall from the Cardigan estate.[15] He had a number of alterations made to the Hall, including the addition of a billiard room (a favourite of the time). He had artistic interests, and was a collector of drawings by the Leeds artist J.N.Rhodes, who had made several sketches of Headingley.[16] The Ingham family remained the owners of the Hall until the 1920s, when it was sold. In the 1940s the Hall was split into two separate residences, but it has now been restored as an entity and adapted to its present use as a residential home. New buildings have been built in the grounds, but the appearance of the old Hall has been partly preserved, and it now boasts a blue plaque recording its ancient origins.

The blue plaque recording the manorial origins of Headingley Hall.

12. For more details see the paper by Charles Timmis, *George Hayward: his Central Asian Explorations, his Murder, his Legacy*, Royal Geographical Society, 1997 (copy in Headingley library).

13. Chosen by Sir Arthur Quiller-Couch for inclusion in *The Oxford Book of English Verse*, 1250–1918, published 1939.

14. A distinguished firm, taken over in 1864 by Marsh and Jones, makers of some of the fine satinwood furniture at Lotherton Hall.

15. Conveyance of 31.10.1884, WR Registry of Deeds, 915.266.

16. For more information on this artist, see William H. Thorp, *John N. Rhodes, A Yorkshire Painter, 1809–1842*, Leeds, 1905.

HEADINGLEY HALL

The medieval manor house of Headingley almost certainly stood here. The Hall was rebuilt in the 17th century and 1831-6. Residents included John Killingbeck, Mayor of Leeds 1677, George Hayward, Land Agent of the Earl of Cardigan, and his son George J.W. Hayward, born here 1839, intrepid explorer in Central Asia.

OTHER 'MANOR HOUSES'

The name Manor House has a prestigious ring and other houses in Headingley have laid claim to it. In the late eighteenth century, a large house was built on the brow of Headingley Lane, next to the present Richmond Road, which was known as the Manor House. It is probable that this house was built for Mary Bainbrigge (née Walker), who inherited the whole of the substantial Walker estate when her sister and co-heir died in 1755. The estate consisted of some 200 acres of land, on both sides of Headingley Lane, between the village and Woodhouse Moor. Mary had married the Rev. Richard Bainbrigge, vicar of Harewood and curate of Chapel Allerton, but was widowed in 1764; she returned to Headingley and may then have had this house built; it was certainly in existence by 1781.[17] She is recorded as living in the house in 1803, when she made her will. She died in 1805 (and is buried at Chapel Allerton), and her estate was divided then into three portions. One portion, including the Manor House with its gardens and orchard, went to her daughter Mary who lived there until her death in 1832. She bequeathed it to her friend Dr Disney Launder Thorp, whose son later put it up for sale. In 1852 this property, comprising the house (by then divided into two and let) and six acres of land, was bought by Anthony Titley, partner in a large flax-spinning firm.[18] He built a fine new house there, which he called the New Manor House, backing onto what is now Richmond Avenue. The Old Manor House, still divided into two residences, was rented out. Both the old and new houses survived until 1900, when the whole estate was sold for redevelopment. The houses were quickly demolished

---

17. Shown on John Tuke's map of the Borough of Leeds, 1781.

18. Titley, Tatham & Walker, established in Hunslet in 1805. Members of the Tatham family already lived in Headingley; Anthony Titley and his family moved from town to live in part of the old Manor House around 1850. He purchased the property on 12.4.1852 (WR Registry of Deeds, RL.308).

Old Manor House
Headingley 1900

W.Braithwaite

and now are remembered only in the names of the 'Manors', the roads which crowd across the former grounds and gardens of the two houses.[19]

Anthony Titley was not the only incomer from town to choose a name for his new house with pretensions to historical grandeur. Across the road, in 1841, the wealthy corn merchant Thomas England built himself an imposing house on land bought from Barbara Marshall, one of the other inheritors of the Walker/Bainbrigge estate.[20] He called his house 'Headingley Castle', and its Gothic design (by the architect John Child) matched the name. Heavily castellated and turreted, it stands in large grounds

The 'Old Manor House' on Headingley Hill, built by Mary Bainbrigge around 1770, in a drawing by Walter Braithwaite dated 1900, just before it was demolished. It stood close to the corner of the present Richmond Road. A 'New Manor House' had been built on adjoining land by Anthony Titley in 1852, which was demolished at the same time. The streets called the Manors were built over their grounds. *(Leeds Library and Information Services)*

---

19. See F. Trowell, 'Speculative Housing Development in the Suburb of Headingley, Leeds, 1838–1914', *PThS* LIX (1985).

20. Title deeds are held by the WYAS Leeds (WYL160/1608 and 2356).

Headingley Castle, built in grandiose Gothic style for the wealthy corn-factor Thomas England in 1841.

shadowed by tall trees (during the nineteenth century it was renamed 'The Elms'). In 1866 it was bought by Arthur Lupton, and from 1908 was occupied by Frank Fulford, the millionaire director of the company selling the hugely successful patent medicine, Bile Beans.[21]

There is another house on the original Walker estate which deserves mention, probably originally a residence of the Walkers or their descendants. This is the fine stone house known as 'The Hollies' at the top of Bainbrigge Road opposite St Michael's Church, half-hidden behind a dry-stone wall of some age. This interesting house was put up for sale in 1869 by the Misses Marshall, descendants of the Walker/Bainbrigge family, together with its stables, coach house and coachman's cottage, all set in extensive gardens and grounds. The sale included the adjoining charming old cottage on the corner, known as Church Cottage. The associated plan showed the grounds divided up into villa plots along the newly-formed Bainbrigge Terrace (now Bainbrigge Road), on Headingley Lane and along one side of Spring Road.[22] Both 'The Hollies' and Church Cottage were bought by James Wilson, a plasterer turned architect who lived in Headingley, father of the better-known architect T. Butler Wilson.[23] Perhaps because of the historical and architectural interests of the Wilsons, these two houses were happily preserved from demolition, unlike many others in this period, destroyed when estates were bought up by speculative builders intent on a quick profit.

---

21. He was a noted collector of objets d'art, some of which are on display at Temple Newsam House. Headingley Castle has now been converted into apartments. When it was first built its entry drive ran from what is now the gate of Hinsley Hall. The intervening fields were part of its grounds, and have since (remarkably) remained undeveloped, providing a view of wild-flower meadows for the passer-by to enjoy.

22. *Particulars of Sale of Freehold Building Sites at Headingley, the property of the Misses Frances and Elizabeth Marshall*, 3.11.1869, WYAS Leeds, AM/1/37.

23. T. Butler Wilson (1859–1942) was the architect responsible for the refurbishment of two fine Headingley houses, Castle Grove and Wheatfields.

'Church Cottage' on Headingley Lane, at the corner with Bainbrigge Road, drawn by Walter Braithwaite in 1900. The spire of the new St. Michael's Church completed in 1890, rises beyond the cottage. The cottage, which still survives although much altered, was in existence in 1781 and may date further back still. *(Leeds Library and Information Services)*

THE HEADINGLEY 'MILLIONAIRE MISER'

One of the plots of land in Headingley Lane offered for sale by the Misses Marshall in 1869 was bought by the reclusive philanthropist Robert Arthington, who was to become widely known as the Headingley Miser, a name he little deserved.[24] He had a large stone house built for himself there, at 57 Headingley Lane, where he was to live until shortly before his death in 1900. He became a familiar figure in the village, dressed in old-fashioned, shabby clothes and an ancient stovepipe hat passed down from his father. He had been born in 1823 to a wealthy Quaker family – his father owned a brewery in Hunslet but gave it up on grounds of conscience – and was educated at Cambridge. He later became a Baptist, and, when he inherited a fortune of over £200,000 on his father's death, he determined to devote the money to good causes, in particular to support missionary work in the previously uncharted areas of Africa, India and China which were then being explored and opened up. It was his passionate wish to spread the gospel to 'the heathen' and, as he saw it, bring light into darkness. Over the years he gave enormous sums to the missionary societies, and also to various charitable purposes closer to home, while he himself chose to live in self-imposed poverty on just a few shillings a week.

What made him move from his Hunslet home to this large new house in Headingley? The story goes that in his late forties he fell in love, and this led him to have a new house built for himself and his hoped-for bride – but he was rejected. True or not, it is clear that from then on he retreated further and further into a strange, isolated life. He lived in only one room, sunless, cold, and thick with dust, and slept there in a chair, wrapped in his coat. He received almost no visitors – people were brusquely turned away. No one saw him smile, and his greeting was always an enquiry after one's soul. He looked after his investments carefully and spent nothing on his own comfort, so his wealth accumulated in spite of all his charitable gifts. When he knew he was dying he gave away over £60,000, including £20,000 to the fund for the Leeds Hospital for Women and Children. In recognition of his gift the new hospital, which opened at Cookridge in 1905, was called the Robert Arthington Hospital (it is now closed). When he died his estate topped £1,000,000. Almost all of it went to the missionary societies with which he had been so closely associated and whose work he had passionately supported. This enormous gift helped to provide hospitals, schools and missions in remote areas in India and Africa, where his name and his generosity are still remembered today.

Robert Arthington, 1823–1900, philanthropist and eccentric, photographed in his younger years before he became a recluse. *(Thoresby Society)*

24. There were many newspaper articles about him, particularly around the time of his death in 1900: see the references in William Benn, 'More Annals of Leeds 1880–1920', *PThS* 2nd Series 15 (2005). Personal recollections of him were recorded by his friend F.R.Spark, in *Memories of my Life*, Leeds, 1913. See also A.M. Chirgwin, *Arthington's Million*, London, 1936. His house still stands in Headingley Lane, turned away from the road, the main door hidden from passers-by.

ST MICHAEL'S CHURCH

EXPANSION AND DISSENT

THE CHURCH WE see now in the heart of the village, standing across the road from its old rivals, the two pubs, dates from the 1880s, but it was not the first church to be built there: there has been a church on this site from the early seventeenth century.[1]

THE 1619 CHAPEL

The ancient parish of Leeds was very extensive and the parish church in the town was difficult for people in outlying villages to get to and too small to accommodate everyone. So from a very early period, small 'chapels of ease' were built in some of the villages to relieve the main church. There are intriguing references that suggest the existence of an medieval chapel in Headingley, perhaps

---

1. Two previous incumbents of Headingley have written histories of St Michael's Church: Canon R.H.Malden, *The Church of Headingley in Four Centuries* (1923); and Canon R.J.Wood, *St Michael's, Headingley* (1957). Both books have provided material for this chapter. The St Michael's parish records are now lodged with the WYAS, Leeds, under ref. RDP39.

Chapel Lane, the old curving bridleway which led up from Burley to Headingley chapel. The chapel served Burley residents until St Matthias church was built in 1854.

dedicated to St Giles,[2] but there is no firm evidence of one. If it existed, it was not on this site. The first chapel there was built in 1619, when James Cotes, a local farmer, 'out of a devout mynd, gave £60 to the building of a convenient chappell for the ease of the inhabitantes'.[3] Sir John Savile, who was Lord of the Manor of Headingley, and his son, Thomas, gave a part of the village green as the site and commissioned the work.[4] The chapel was to serve the people of the whole township, including the neighbouring villages of Burley and Kirkstall as well as Headingley itself – the narrow lane which led up to the chapel from Burley is still called Chapel Lane. On 19 January 1627 the Archbishop of York issued a licence for 'the new chapel at Headingley', so presumably by then a minister had been appointed. Almost certainly from its inauguration, the chapel was dedicated to St Michael.[5]

This first chapel was a low, modest building less than 70 feet long, about the same size as the small church which still survives at Adel. There was no tower, just a belfry. It could hold just over 200 people, adequate for its time. Initially it had little in the way of endowments, and indeed was one of the poorer of the village chapels around Leeds, its income less than half that of the chapels at Beeston, Armley and Bramley. When inspected by the Archdeacon of York in 1723, it was found wanting in several respects: the curate was told to clear the churchyard of rubbish, and

2. The Skyrack Subsidy Roll of 1327 refers to a chaplain with a house in Headingley, and a will of 1522 talks of the church 'of Sayncte Giles of Heddingley'(Will of Thomas Benson, 25.10.1522, G.D.Lumb, ed., 'Testamenta Leodiensia', *PThS* IX, p.247 (1899)).

3. Notes made by Roger Dodsworth, the Yorkshire antiquary, in 1619: *YAS Record Series* XXXIV.

4. The deed dated 15 September 1619 conveying the ground where 'a new Chappell is lately erected' to trustees, who were also to provide a 'good learned minister or clergyman to read and celebrate divine service', is recorded in the Return made by the Leeds Commissioners to the Archbishop of York in 1716: *PThS* XXVI (1924) p.165.

5. Not St Giles, as has been suggested. John Ecton's *Thesaurus Rerum Ecclesiasticorum*, 1742, calls the chapel 'Heddingley St Michael'; there is no reason to suppose that there had been any change.

provide a 'carpet' for the communion table, together with 'a linnen cloth, a flagon and paten and a bason for the offertory'. However, in the late seventeenth and eighteenth centuries the chapel benefited from a number of endowments and gifts of plate from local worthies, notably the Wades of New Grange, John Walker (Recorder of Leeds 1711–1729), and John Killingbeck of Headingley Hall. In 1737, when the curate of Headingley was also appointed to serve as vicar of Calverley (near enough for a man with a good horse), the living was further augmented by a substantial gift from that great benefactress Lady Elizabeth Hastings, Lord of the Manor of Calverley, in the form of tithe rents from land.

THE PARSONAGE

One of the gifts to the chapel in 1717 was a parsonage house at Burley: a large house with seven bedrooms but quite a distance from the chapel. Some 50 years later action was taken to provide a newer and more convenient house for the curate and at the same time augment the glebe land belonging to the chapel. Around 1770, 41 acres of the common land on Headingley Moor were enclosed with the permission of the Lord of the Manor, the Duke of Montague (the Earl of Cardigan's senior title at that time), and the other major landowners, for the benefit of the curate.[6] This was a large swathe of the Moor, about a third of its acreage, running (in modern terms) from Shaw Lane almost up to Cottage Road – a substantial gift (at no cost to the donors). A new parsonage was built there in 1770, of stone and slate, with brick stabling behind, four rooms on each floor, flagged or deal floors, and plastered walls with no wainscotting[7] – a fairly simple, austere residence,

The parsonage built for the curate of Headingley in 1770 on land which had been part of Headingley Moor: 41 acres of the Moor were granted in 1770 as glebe land. The house was substantially extended to the side (on the right in this photograph) around 1850. The surrounding glebe land was sold in 1874, when Burton Crescent was created, and the house was sold in 1884 as it was then outside the parish of St Michael's.

6. There may well have been resentment about the loss of this common land to the church. A proposal in 1790 to enclose some further land for the benefit of the curate was never proceeded with, apparently because of action by local people, who repeatedly pulled up the fencing. (WYAS Leeds, WYL160/220/196)

7. WYAS Leeds, RDP39/37, 1770 Terrier (inventory of lands).

The new vicarage for St Michael's, built in 1887 in the prestigious new Shire Oak Road. This large house was designed to reflect the status of the vicar of the 'proud and prosperous' new church of St Michael's, consecrated just the year before.

later extended and enhanced. This house, now called Holly Dene, still stands on Otley Road and is currently used as a dental surgery. It remained the parsonage until 1884, when it was sold as it now fell within the new parish of St Chad's. A new vicarage for St Michael's was built in Shire Oak Road on a much larger and grander scale to match its wealthy neighbours and reflect the status of the vicar: four maidservants were needed to keep it going.[8]

The Old Chapel

In 1782 John Smithson was appointed curate of Headingley and served for nearly 54 years. During much of the time he was also rector of Kirkheaton, near Huddersfield, so he employed an assistant at Headingley and was seldom there. However, when he died in 1836 aged 83, he bequeathed a sum of £100 for the poor of Headingley, and there is a brass plate to him and his wife in the centre aisle of the present church. His long curacy bridged the period when the old village of Headingley, with its established population and ways of life, was giving way to the new developments and changes of the early nineteenth century. Inevitably, while he remained in post, little was done to bring the chapel up to date or to adjust to the surrounding changes.

There are several references to the old chapel in the diary of Thomas Butler of Kirkstall Forge, a lively and engaging account of his youthful activities in the years 1796–99,[9] and they help to give a picture of its place in local people's lives. In addition to Sunday services, it was the place for some of the 'Town' meetings, when matters such as the maintenance of the chapel, the management of the charity school, the supervision of the recently

8. This house was sold in 1945; since then two other houses in Shire Oak Road have served in turn as the vicarage. Currently there is no incumbent in residence.

9. *The Diary of Thomas Butler of Kirkstall Forge, Yorkshire, 1796–1799*, published privately, 1906.

formed Sunday School, and the distribution of funds for the poor were discussed and decided. It is clear from his comments that the chapel had by this time become far too small to serve all the residents of the township, and many people 'had no right in the chapel on account of having no sittings'. The pressure on places led to arguments: he comments that his family had been in dispute with the parson for several years over their right to a particular pew. If the situation was bad in 1799, it was to become much worse as time went on.

While we know what the old chapel looked like outside, there is no picture of its interior, but some memories of what it was like around 1827 were recorded in 1890.[10] It was of very rough construction; the roof was open to the rafters, the timber unpainted; the pulpit, a low three-decker, extended from the north wall to the aisle, and the pews were the old box kind, with doors.

Headingley Chapel (1619–1837), viewed from the north-east. The chapel was built on part of the village green, on a site granted by Sir John Savile, Lord of the Manor. A local farmer, John Cotes, gave £60 towards the building, and the chapel was licensed for services in 1627. This simple chapel, dedicated to St Michael, served the people of Headingley, Burley and Kirkstall for over 200 years. *(Leeds Library and Information Services)*

10. *Yorkshire Weekly Post*, 27.12.1890. The writer's memories may be shaky, as in fact a ceiling had been put in below the open raftered roof ('underdrawing') in 1799.

The churchyard at
St Michael's was extended
by this piece of common land
bought in the enclosure sale
in 1831. In 1874 the churchyard
was closed and burials
then took place at the new
Lawnswood cemetery.
The house overlooking the
churchyard belonged in
the early 19th century to the
parish clerk and overseer
of the poor, Benjamin Brooke
– a good spot to keep an eye
on everything going on.

The parish clerk, Benjamin Brooke, sat in front of the pulpit, inserting psalm and hymn numbers into a box with a great clatter and turning the box round with a stick for the guidance of the congregation. There were two professional singers to lead the hymns, paid £1 a quarter. Music was provided by a seraphine, a sort of harmonium, the performer and instrument set among the pews, surrounded by scarlet curtains.

The only change during this period was the purchase of some land to extend the graveyard, bought in the enclosure sales of 1831. Otherwise the old low chapel, its floor sunk below ground level and increasingly dilapidated, remained unchanged until the death of Mr Smithson in 1836.

OVERSEER OF THE POOR

In the 1830s and 40s Benjamin Brooke, the schoolmaster and parish clerk, acted as assistant Overseer of the Poor for the township of Headingley. The township was part of the vast Carlton Poor Law Union, formed in 1818 (a 'Gilbert' Union), which consisted of 40 townships both within and outside the Borough of Leeds, stretching from the southeast round the inner township and out through Adel, Otley and Ilkley along Wharfedale (the township of Leeds itself was separate). The Union workhouse where paupers from Headingley would be sent was a barracks-like building far away over the fields at East Carlton, an isolated hamlet near the top of the Chevin on the fringe of Guiseley – conditions there were later described as 'as bad as can be'.[11] In 1841 when the census was taken, 91 people were housed there, 26 of them children under ten.

11. There are records of the Carlton Workhouse in the Otley Museum collection, O/WU/dc/1and 2.

Benjamin Brooke had a position of power. He was responsible for collecting the poor rate from households assessed as eligible, along with other local rates, and he controlled how the money was doled out. People in need had to apply to him for relief and he took the decision how much to give them (the minimum feasible); whether they could be found work, perhaps breaking stones on the road; or whether they should be sent to the workhouse. Those unable to work, the old, the sick, and the mentally ill, usually finished up in the workhouse, though the Overseers also rented two small cottages in Far Headingley which could be used to house suitable paupers. He decided questions relating to 'settlement' affecting the poor in Headingley – which parish or township should be held legally responsible for their support – and when necessary he would escort them back there. He also dealt with issues relating to destitute children born out of wedlock, when action had to be taken to pursue the putative father and force him to pay for the child, on pain of imprisonment. In general he took a hard line, though Headingley did not suffer the terrible problems of some of the manu-facturing areas subject to periodic trade depressions and unemployment, and the poor rates were consequently low (a good selling point for local property).

In 1832 a Royal Commission was appointed to investigate the operation of the Poor Laws and make recommendations for reform; Benjamin Brooke was among those interviewed and his evidence was printed in the Commissioners' Report,[12] providing an insight into the attitudes and methods of the time. The Poor Law Amendment Act was passed in 1834, but it did not affect the administration of the Carlton Union directly: change was resisted. However, the new Poor Law Commissioners could and did intervene in special cases. In February 1843 Benjamin Brooke earned an official reprimand for his 'alleged cruelty' to a pauper, Jonathan Brooksbank, and his wife: 'harshness of manner and severity of language are to be avoided...' he was told.[13] In 1869, after the break-up of the Carlton Union, Headingley was incorporated into the Leeds Union, together with the adjoining townships in the Borough. The workhouse at Carlton, described as 'wholly inadequate and unsufficient in every respect', was demolished. No trace of it remains.

12. Report of the Commissioners of the Poor Laws, 1832, J.D. Tweedy, Appendix A, p.495.

13. *Leeds Mercury* 18.2.1843.

THE SECOND CHURCH: RESPONDING TO DISSENT

After Mr Smithson's death in 1836, William Williamson, curate and lecturer at Leeds Parish Church, was appointed curate at Headingley. He was well qualified and energetic, in his middle thirties, evangelical in his approach and keen to play an active role in Headingley – quite a change from his elderly and frequently absent predecessor. When he and his wife arrived in Headingley, it was to find that a growing number of the local community were dissenters, some belonging to the older chapels of the town, others meeting in Headingley itself, right under the nose of the church: just two years before, a new Wesleyan chapel had been built just round the corner (in what is now King's Place, off St Michael's Road). Furthermore, the new curate faced serious problems of accommodation. The old chapel was much too small, in desperate need of repair, and too dilapidated to be extended. All the pews had long ago been allocated to named owners paying pew rents, leaving no room for new arrivals or for the poorer inhabitants of the area. Although a new church, St Stephen's, had been built at Kirkstall in 1829, the old chapel continued to be the only centre of worship for the villages of Burley, Headingley itself, and Far Headingley, and the population was growing. The only solution was to start afresh with a new building. A committee of influential local residents was set up immediately.

This was a time when the Anglican Church had become increasingly aware of the need to reach out to the mass of the people and to bring them into the Church, in the face of the growing popularity of the dissenting movements, which were actively recruiting new converts in the urban areas. In Leeds this resurgence was reflected in a scheme to provide more churches, with free places for the poor. The proposal to build afresh in Headingley fitted well with these objectives and permission was given for a new chapel with 600 sittings, of which at least 130 were to be free – not a large proportion, one might feel now, but a

significant opening up of the church in comparison with the past. Action followed quickly.

The old chapel which had served Headingley for over 200 years was demolished,[14] and the foundation stone of the new church was laid in April 1837, with 'a considerable number of the inhabitants of Headingley' joining in the hymns and prayers.[15] As the new church began to rise it must have seemed a symbol of the new age heralded by the accession of Queen Victoria in June that year, amid much celebration. The church was consecrated on 31 January

The second church: Headingley St Michael's, 1838–1885. A new church was needed in 1838 to accommodate the growing population of Headingley and to provide free places for the poor. The architect was Robert Dennis Chantrell, architect of Leeds Parish Church. Although much larger than the old chapel, the new church was deemed too small almost from the start. This drawing by W.R. Robinson was made c1840, shortly after the new church had opened. *(Leeds Library and Information Services)*

14. It is said that some of the wood was later used to make two chairs (dated 1870) still to be seen in the present church.

15. WYAS Leeds, RDP39/84, Minutes of the Building Committee.

1838 in the presence of Dr Longley, the new Bishop of Ripon,[16] and Dr Hook, who had just been appointed Vicar of Leeds and was at the start of his 22 years of energetic and charismatic service in Leeds. The architect was Robert Dennis Chantrell (1793–1872) who, in that same period 1837–1838, was working with Hook on ambitious plans for the rebuilding of the Parish Church in Leeds, a project which was designed to revitalise the Church and bring honour to the town. He was already well known in the West Riding and had been responsible for a number of other churches, including St Stephen's at Kirkstall. Trained in Sir John Soane's office in London, he was an expert in Gothic church design. While his Parish Church remains today an impressive and distinguished monument to his achievements and to Dr Hook's vision, his church in Headingley was destined to stand only some 50 years.

The cost of the new chapel, £2,582, was met entirely by local subscription. Of the many new churches built in Leeds at this period, only one other was funded without the aid of grants from Parliament or from the Diocese, a measure of the commitment and deep pockets of the local residents. William Beckett of New Grange and Lord Cardigan as Lord of the Manor both gave substantial donations, and other residents made up the rest. Even the architect himself, Chantrell, contributed half his commission, a sum of £59 2s. 6d. John Mayhall, in his *Annals of Yorkshire* (1866), gives a muted description of the building: 'Headingley Church near Leeds, dedicated to St Michael, is a neat cruciform structure in the latter English style, with an embattled tower surmounted by a graceful spire'. Its peal of bells was taken over from the old Leeds Parish Church, and for the next 50 years these bells, cast in 1798, summoned the residents of Headingley to worship.[17]

---

16. The Ripon diocese had been formed just over a year earlier, at the end of 1836. Dr Longley was later to become Archbishop of Canterbury.

17. The metal was later used to make a new peal for the present church, so this historical connection has not been entirely lost.

Not Enough Room

Although the new church was much larger than the old one, a bitter row broke out immediately over the allocation of pews. It had been agreed that all the pewholders in the old church would be allocated pews and then places would be allotted to new subscribers. The right to a pew and its position in the church was jealously guarded and fought for. In addition, the provision of 130 free sittings for the poor had to be respected. In the event some of these were on benches rather than pews, an arrangement which was objected to as demeaning but was nevertheless put into effect.[18] Disputes broke out, no agreement could be reached, and in the end it became necessary for the church authorities to appoint Commissioners to determine the allocation of pews among all those who claimed a place – so central was the church in the life of the community.

During the 1840s, not long after the building of the new church, action was taken through two Acts of Parliament to break up the vast ancient parish of Leeds into a number of smaller, more manageable parishes which would reflect the growth and new distribution of the population. In 1849 the chapelry of Headingley-cum-Burley was constituted a separate ecclesiastical parish, which meant that the chapel could now be called a church and the curate could have the title of vicar. St Stephen's, Kirkstall, had already been hived off to form a separate parish in 1829, and subsequent changes reduced the size of St Michael's parish through the building of new churches with their own parishes: St Matthias, Burley (1854), St Chad's, Far Headingley (1866) and St Augustine's, Wrangthorn (1869). However, the population served by St Michael's continued to expand rapidly and overcrowding remained a problem; indeed, within a couple of years the new church was declared to be far too small for its congregation.

---

18. WYAS Leeds, RDP 39/84.

Correspondence in 1843 gives a flavour of the time: 60 seats had been put aside for the Sunday Scholars, but there were over 90 Sunday Scholars and usually more than 80 came to church each week, Sunday School being the only place of instruction in reading and writing available to many children. Some had been put in the seats reserved for the poor but this had caused complaints (even, it was said, used as an excuse for not attending church).[19] There was no easy solution, and overcrowding remained an issue which in due course had to be addressed.

Meanwhile, the energetic Mr Williamson became involved in other disputes. One concerned the payment of the church rate, a compulsory rate based on the value of property which had to be paid by local residents alongside rates for the poor, the upkeep of the highways, etc. The church rate went towards church expenses: heating, lighting, and general maintenance of the building and the graveyard. Of course, dissenters objected to paying the rate and in 1843–44 Mr Williamson took action against Quakers in Headingley for non-payment,[20] at a time when elsewhere the rate was lapsing or becoming voluntary. This must have caused considerable resentment and it is clear that it subsequently became increasingly difficult for the churchwardens to collect the rate from unwilling people.[21] In the same period, in 1843, Mr Williamson was involved in a dispute over the running of the Town School next door to the church. Mr. Williamson and 'his womenfolk' were accused of interfering in the affairs of the school and had upset the schoolmaster and also George Hayward, Lord Cardigan's agent, who was

19. WYAS Leeds, RDP39/127. Letters from John Hope Shaw.

20. Harry W. Dalton, 'Anglican Resurgence under W.F.Hook in Early Victorian Leeds', *PThS* 2nd Series 12 (2001) p 137.

21. This led in 1851 to one of the Headingley churchwardens, Reid Newsome, publishing a pamphlet proposing changes in the law: *A Proposal for an Alteration in the law of Church Rates ...* (copy in Leeds Local Studies Library). It is not clear that Parliament ever considered his proposal, but the problem was well recognised and compulsory church rates were abolished in 1868.

then one of the School trustees. The chairman, John Hope Shaw, had to intervene to smooth things over (see p.131).

Fortunately the Williamsons had another outlet for their educational interests, as a few years before, in 1840, they had been active in the founding of a new infants' school, the Glebe School, on the glebe land just beyond the vicarage where they lived (near the present Burton Crescent). It was for the education of poor children on National Society principles and came directly under the management of the vicar. Apparently Mrs Williamson took a very active interest in it, so avoiding conflict with other local interests. She was also closely involved with the setting up of the nearby Headingley Orphan Homes.

The Parochial Institute – Promoting 'Improvement'

The vicar made use of the Glebe School building to further his interest in education and improvement by setting up a parochial lending library there, with over 200

The carving over the porch of the (St Michael's) Parochial Institute, opened in Bennett Road in 1884, designed by George Corson. It shows St Michael slaying the dragon. The Institute offered a large hall, a reading room, billiards and other facilities for young working men.

volumes. The catalogue still survives,[22] with its list of improving texts: no light reading here. The subscription was 1s. a year, but free to Sunday School teachers. The Glebe School was also the base for the Headingley Mutual Improvement Society, founded in 1849 with a view to providing evening lectures and study opportunities for young working men.[23] The Glebe School was closed after the new parish of St Chad's was formed in 1866 as it was then outside the boundary of St Michael's, and the building was sold in 1875 (and later demolished). The money was spent in purchasing a site in Bennett Road for the building of a new Parochial Institute, also dedicated to providing opportunities for education and self-improvement for working people. The Institute building, designed by George Corson, still stands in Bennett Road, notable for its tall church-like window and sculpted porch. When the Institute was opened in June 1884, the Mayor welcomed the opportunities it offered 'for self-improvement and wholesome recreation' for local young men who might otherwise be 'loafing around the streets' or going to the pubs. It had a reading room with the daily newspapers, and a large lecture theatre/meeting room, which Headingley had previously lacked.[24]

---

22. R. Wood, *Notes on the Headingley Parochial Lending Library*, (Leeds Local Studies Library).

23. *Leeds Mercury*, 2.2.1850. J.G. Marshall, John Hope Shaw and William Beckett were all supporters. The Headingley Society followed the lead of the Leeds Mutual Improvement Society formed in 1844, inspired by the teaching of Samuel Smiles (author in 1859 of the bestseller *Self-Help*) who came to address them and praised the work of such societies in 'elevating and improving' the working classes. In 1860 the Headingley Society had 82 members, paying 2s. 6d.–10s. p.a.

24. *Leeds Mercury*, 13.6.1884. Later a billiard room was added, and facilities for badminton, but membership dwindled in the twentieth century, with the competition from the cinemas and other entertainments. After the Second World War the British Legion occupied part of the building and other rooms were used for various community activities, but in 1984 it was sold and converted to offices. More details are to be found in R.H.Malden, *A Short History of the Parochial Institute* (WYAS Leeds, RDP39/198).

FURTHER CONFLICT

From 1869 onwards, the church was involved in an increasingly bitter dispute over the best way of dealing with the problem of overcrowding. A scheme was devised to extend the building but it proved impossible to gain much extra space without disturbing graves, which was viewed as unacceptable. Another proposal was to construct a mission room near the top of Shaw Lane but this was opposed by the then Vicar of Leeds, Dr Gott, on grounds of expense. He suggested holding two services on a Sunday morning, one 'for artisans' and a later one for the upper classes, a divisive suggestion totally rejected by the vicar of Headingley, who accused Dr Gott and his 'secret abettors' of conspiring against him. No immediate solution was found.

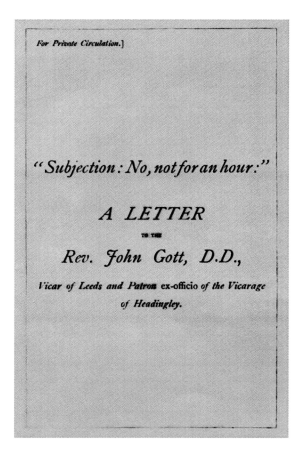

This open letter was written and circulated in 1881 by Samuel Hatch of Oak Lodge, Headingley, protesting at the appointment of Frederick Wood as vicar of Headingley on the grounds that he was a 'Romaniser'.
(Thoresby Society)

The appointment of a new vicar of Headingley in 1881 was the cause of further agitation among local residents. Frederick Wood had been assistant curate at Leeds Parish Church for 25 years and, as might be expected from this background, was known to be very high church. There was considerable dismay in Headingley when his appointment was announced from those who feared the 'Romanising' of services. Samuel Hatch of Oak Lodge published an open letter to Dr Gott raising his objections, under the fervent title 'Subjection: No, Not for an Hour'. But it was in vain. Wood was appointed, and seems to have proceeded fairly cautiously in introducing liturgical changes, though John Hepper, the wealthy estate agent who lived at 'Clareville' in Cardigan Road, recorded his 'deep grief' at the alterations made to the Communion table (probably the introduction of a cross and candlesticks, then viewed by many traditional Anglicans as a rather shocking innovation).

Wood tackled the issue of overcrowding straight away and pressed for the building of a new church. He called together a number of prominent residents of the parish and a committee was formed to push the project through. In 1882 an architect was appointed: John Loughborough Pearson (1817–97), a distinguished man with a national reputation in church architecture, responsible for Truro Cathedral (1879) and a number of churches in London and elsewhere. (Local architects were understandably annoyed at being disregarded.) A public meeting was called in September 1882 to launch the scheme for a new church, but opposition was gathering, dividing local opinion and arousing intense feeling.

A Deepening Divide

Opponents of the scheme held a rival public meeting at the Oak inn on 4 September, and subsequently put a notice in the *Yorkshire Post* [25] headed 'Proposed Desecration of

---

25. *Yorkshire Post*, 30.4.1883.

Headingley Churchyard', claiming support from nearly 300 'leading resident householders'. They argued that there was no need for a new church; that in any case alternative sites existed; that building on the present site would mean the desecration of graves; and that the disturbance of graves would cause a pestilence. The case went before the Chancellor of the Diocese on 25 and 26 June 1883, and evidence was heard from both sides, including the results of numerous borings in the churchyard to establish the presence or otherwise of human remains. The objectors' case was dismissed: the new church was to go ahead. However, the protests continued in an alarmingly bitter atmosphere; a pamphlet was printed and circulated in August 1883,[26] accusing the vicar and his churchwardens of 'gross and outrageous misstatements' and claiming strong support, notably from Dr Albutt, who predicted that 'if once the graveyard is disturbed an epidemic of diphtheria, putrid sore throat, or typhoid fever will break out in the immediate neighbourhood of the church, and thence will be conveyed by contagion to the other parts of Headingley.' It is said that the objectors even displayed placards headed 'Traffic in Dead Bodies', asserting that the vicar was planning to sell exhumed bodies for his own profit. There were threats to burn down the new vicarage, and one resident remembered in later years a youthful plot to arrange a fatal accident for the vicar by fixing a tripwire across the vicarage path. Whatever the truth, feelings were running high. There was much talk of an appeal but in the end this was dropped, possibly because of the expense or just from protest fatigue. So the building of the new church went ahead. In 1884 the foundation stone was laid and the old church was closed and demolished. Some graves had to be moved; no pestilence occurred.

---

26. Pamphlet: *Proposed Desecration of the Churchyard of St. Michael's, Headingley,* (Leeds Local Studies Library).

The Present Church

In July 1886 the new church was consecrated, though the tower was not completed until four years later. The final cost was almost £20,000, all met by subscription, though it took a considerable time to collect the full amount needed. The new church held around 800 people, 200 more than the previous church, and all the places were free. The new building was much admired. The guidebook *Through Airedale, from Goole to Malham* (1891), describes getting off the tram at the old Shire Oak tree, and then 'Over the way towers the magnificent new church of St Michael, unquestionably one of the noblest examples of its style (thirteenth century) in England.' Pevsner, while devoting little space to the church, called it 'proud and prosperous'.[27] While in retrospect it seems a sad waste of resources to have demolished Chantrell's church after only 50 years in order to build again for the sake of 200 more places, this extravagant act can be seen as symbolic of the confidence of the period in a secure and stable future and in the continuing expansion and loyalty to the church of this well-heeled and comfortable suburb.

Proud and prosperous the new church was: the last years of the century and the early years of the twentieth century were a golden era for the church. It was enriched with numerous gifts from wealthy local residents, notably a new organ from Charles Francis Tetley,[28] who served as churchwarden for 53 years and was a generous benefactor; the tower clock (by Potts & Sons), to which eyes still turn to check the time, given by the industrialist Sir Arthur

27. N. Pevsner, *The Buildings of England: Yorkshire West Riding*, Penguin, 1959. A much fuller description of the church appears in the new *Pevsner Architectural Guide to Leeds* by Susan Wrathmell (2005).

28. Charles Francis Tetley (1849–1934), Chairman of Tetleys Breweries 1902-1934, Lord Mayor of Leeds 1897, Freeman of the City, a strong supporter of the church, a patron of the arts, with a keen interest in education. He lived at Spring Bank, Headingley Lane, from 1890 until 1912 when he moved to Fox Hill, Weetwood.

Lawson of Weetwood Hall; the stained glass windows; and many other fine fittings throughout the church and valuable items of plate, from a wide range of donors. The church was a focal point for the neighbourhood. A local resident recording her memories of the early years of the century recalled how all the people 'from the big houses' drove in their landaus to St Michael's Church every Sunday, to the clatter of hooves over the cobbles.[29]

In the twentieth century the church was enhanced with further gifts. It contains some fine woodwork by Robert Thompson of Kilburn, the 'Mouseman', and houses the small madonna which he carved from the wood of the old

The present church of St Michael's, 'proud and prosperous' in a photograph from around 1903. The Oak in its railed enclosure on the left still bears some leaves at a low level. The poles for the new (1900) electric tramway are in place; the white paint on the pole further on to the left signifies the tram stop. Tramlines can be seen cutting through the setts of the road, but horses are still the common means of private travel.

29. Article on Ivy Lodge, *Yorkshire Evening Post*, 23.11.1967.

Shire Oak after it collapsed in 1941. The church remains a landmark in the heart of the old village, but over the last century it seems to have mostly lost the battle for young hearts and minds to its old competitors opposite.[30]

The Wesleyans

St Michael's was not the only church expanding and building in Headingley in the nineteenth century. In the 1820s there was an active group of Wesleyans in the village, led by a woollen draper from the town, Robert Dewsbury, and meeting in a room in a cottage near the Skyrack pub.[31] When a few plots of land in the centre of the village came up for sale in June 1831 as part of the enclosure procedure, they seized the opportunity to buy a plot next to the Town School in St Michael's Road (where King's Place is now), in order to build a chapel. The purchaser on behalf of the group was Samuel Holmes, a linen merchant, who at the same time bought land outside the village along the newly-formed Moor Road and built a fine house for himself: Castle Grove.[32] He was one of the chapel trustees with Robert Dewsbury, who also made the move from his home in town, in St James' Street, to live in Headingley. He bought land on the Moor at the corner of Moor Road and Shaw Lane, where he built a terrace of four houses around 1846, aptly called Wesley Terrace. It is still there, one of the first of the stone terraces to be built on plots on the Moor after enclosure.

The chapel the Wesleyans built was a plain rectangular building in stone. When it ceased to be used in 1845 it was converted into two houses which can still be seen in King's

---

30. The churchyard currently suffers from problems of litter and vandalism, in spite of heroic efforts by church helpers to look after it. At the back it is sadly overgrown: as it is no longer in use, its care is the responsibility of Leeds City Council.

31. See J. Stanley Mathers, *A History of Headingley Methodism*, Leeds, 1970.

32. For the story of Castle Grove, see E.R. Vaughan, *A History of Castle Grove 1834–1994*, Leeds, 1996.

Place and reflect its original size and shape. This small chapel was in use for over ten years, but by 1840 it was felt to be much too small for the growing congregation of Wesleyans in Headingley and a site for a new church was sought. Two years were spent trying to find a suitable site and in the end the building committee approached George Hayward, the agent for the Cardigan estate, with a request to intercede on their behalf with Lord Cardigan, as he owned most of the available land in the village. This he did, perhaps influenced by his wife, who was a Wesleyan, and after some problems over price agreement was finally reached on a site on the edge of the village, just beyond the toll bar at North Lane corner.[33] Authority was given for building to start straight away, and the new chapel was completed and formally opened in July 1845. It was and is an imposing building in Gothic style, the first chapel in Leeds to move away from the simpler structures of the past. The new church of St Michael's had opened on the other side of the village in 1838, and perhaps the Wesleyan community felt a need to have a building which could match it and be a visible symbol of their strength and commitment. The chapel was extended in 1857 by the addition of a Sunday School, and extended again in 1862, but, as with St Michael's, overcrowding remained a problem, and all the pews were soon occupied, leaving little room for new arrivals. Further additions to the building were made, and finally in 1908 a new School was built on the Chapel Street side, to provide space for all those who wanted to come. So the building assumed more or less the appearance it has today.

But the landscape of course has changed completely. When the chapel was built in 1845, it was surrounded by fields and just a scatter of cottages on the corner of North Lane and along the Leeds-Otley turnpike road. Within the next twenty years, however, after the Cardigan estate sales of 1850 onwards, Chapel Street, Chapel Square

The Wesleyan chapel, opened in Otley Road in 1845, and later substantially extended.

---

33. Minutes of the Quarterly Meetings of the Leeds Second Circuit, Oxford Place Chapel, 1841-44, WYAS Leeds, OP9.

and Chapel Place were created, their small close-packed cottages clustered round the chapel. Across the road to the front, the view initially was of fields running up to the Ridge, with the pinfold for stray cattle and livestock opposite, together with the toll house and gate for the turnpike road. Later, in the 1860s, three large villas were built there, Alma House, Aysgarth and St Ronans, standing grandly in their leafy gardens, and towards the end of the century the grounds of the Headingley Lawn Tennis Club extended behind them, its entrance at the corner with Wood Lane. In the 1960s the houses, gardens and tennis courts were all cleared away and the Arndale Centre, opened in 1965, constructed in their place: a brutal change of view.

The view in 1964 of the Wesleyan chapel from across the Otley Road, after the site of the future Arndale Centre had been cleared of the three houses which had stood there in their wooded gardens, with the courts of the Headingley Tennis Club behind. The Arndale Centre was opened in 1965. *(Thoresby Society)*

HEADINGLEY WESLEYAN COLLEGE

An object of local pride, particularly for the Wesleyan community, was the Headingley Wesleyan College in Headingley Lane, which opened in September 1868.[34] In the early 1860s the national Wesleyan Conference had begun to look for a site in the north of England to build a new establishment for the training of its ministers. Various possible locations had been considered and investigated, but in 1866 it was announced that 'an eligible site, on elevated ground, in a salubrious district' had been found at Headingley. Approval was given to the purchase and a building committee appointed. Architects from Bath were chosen for the work (Cuthbert Brodrick also submitted a design, which was rejected) and they produced a strangely exotic building, crowned with a sort of onion dome (strictly a conical tower above a colonnade). The college was to become a favourite subject for postcards at the turn of the century and remains today a surprising sight when glimpsed through the trees or from the bus. The choice of Headingley was not regretted: according to one commentator, while the college was within sight and sound of the furnaces and steam hammers of the city at night, and touched by its sooty atmosphere, its air was 'bracing and invigorating' and its position, set in its large grounds, 'suitable and most healthy'.[35] The College was designed to accommodate 40 students, candidates for the Wesleyan ministry (it was later extended to take 60), together with teaching staff. No expense was spared; the total cost was £30,000, mostly found from central funds but also by subscriptions raised locally and throughout the north. At the opening ceremony the newly appointed Governor pointed out that the college was 'in the very heart of the Methodism of the district' and 'afforded abundant opportunities for the evangelistic labours of the students'. The students were expected to take part in missionary work in and around Leeds and had strong links with the local Wesleyan community.

During the First World War the College had to close from 1916 and only reopened much later in 1930. In the Second World War it closed again in 1943 when the building was taken over by the WRNS. It reopened in 1946 but closed finally in 1967, when it merged with Didsbury College, Bristol. However, under the name of Hinsley Hall the building has now found a new use not totally unrelated to its past, as a Pastoral and Conference Centre for the Roman Catholic Diocese of Leeds.

---

34. A history of the College is to be found in the final edition of the College magazine *The Ark*, no. 16, 1967. (Thoresby Society)

35. *Wesleyan Methodist Magazine*, October 1906, article by J.E.Hellier (Special Collections, University of Leeds).

The Wesleyan College, opened in September 1868, was an object of pride for the Wesleyan community locally and nationally. It was a training college for Wesleyan ministers, one of only five in the country and the first to be built from scratch, with no expense spared. Headingley was chosen for its healthy, elevated position and the supportive local community. This postcard view dates from the early 1900s.

HIDDEN COTTAGES

ST MICHAEL'S COTTAGE, ST MICHAEL'S LANE

THIS IS ONE of several old cottages left in Headingley village, mostly tucked away and shielded from view. Their history is often obscure, for the homes and lives of ordinary villagers go mostly unrecorded. However, this particular cottage can be traced back fairly well, and its story tells us something of the old agricultural life of the village and how it was affected by the sweeping changes of the middle and late nineteenth century.

The cottage in its present setting stands back at an angle from St Michael's Lane, with a secluded woodland garden in front. Its uneven walls of random stone are a foot and a half thick, and show signs of earlier alterations. Inside, the oak beams, low ceilings and stone staircase speak of its age. Outside there are clear signs that it once was larger, with buildings to each side. While the way to the cottage is now from St Michael's Lane, there was no road there originally: the outlook in front was over the garden, the fields beyond, and then down the wooded slopes towards Kirkstall and the river.

The cottage is early eighteenth century in origin, perhaps even older. It was built close to what was then the heart of the old village, near the chapel, on land which belonged to the Lord of the Manor, the Earl of Cardigan.

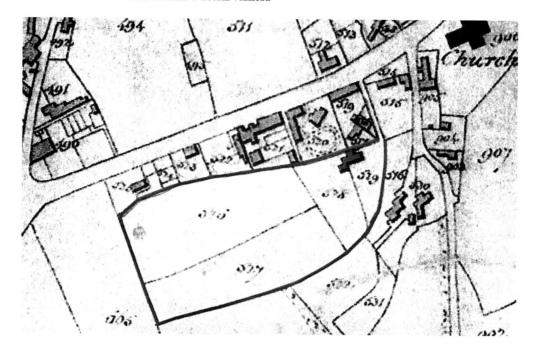

Extract from the 1846 Tithe Map showing Joshua Hillas's cottage, now known as St Michael's Cottage, with the fields which made up this small farm outlined in red. The farm had remained almost unchanged since the early eighteenth century. *(National Archives, Kew)*

It looks as though it was already in existence in 1711, as a house in roughly this position is shown on the Cardigan estate map of that date. The map shows the house standing, with a second house behind,[1] in what is called a 'garth' – a piece of enclosed land, a garden or allotment, usually next to a house. This land, together with two adjoining fields called Near Butt Close and Far Butt Close, and another small field called Pinfold Close across the lane to Kirkstall (which probably contained the village pinfold where stray animals were rounded up) were all rented to a John Denison, making a smallholding of just over four acres.

The records show that this farm continued in the tenancy of the Denison family until 1775 on a series of 21-year leases, which was the customary term for farms on the estate. There were several such smallholdings around the

1. The second house is almost certainly the old cottage which still stands behind St Michael's Cottage, tucked away in its garden at the end of King's Place. In the nineteenth century it was known as Dean's Cottage, and it is thought to date from the seventeenth century or even earlier.

village. In 1775 the lease was taken over by John Newland, at a yearly rent of £7 12s. However, he died three years later in 1778, and the farm passed to his son-in-law Samuel Hillas, who had married John Newland's daughter Mary in 1782. By trade Samuel was a carpenter, but in this still predominantly agricultural area it was quite usual for people to combine running a small farm with other work. The survey of the Cardigan estate made in 1792–8[2] lists Samuel as tenant still of two cottages, with a barn and garth, and three fields totalling over six acres: a mix of pasture, meadow and arable land. His rent had gone up to £22 p.a., again on a 21-year lease. While two cottages are still listed in this survey, the second one, Dean's cottage, was later divided off and rented out separately, together with its enclosed garden, some time early in the nineteenth century.[3]

Samuel Hillas continued to rent the main cottage and the adjoining fields from the Cardigan estate for some 45 years and ran his farm until his death in 1830, aged 83. He had two sons, John Newland (baptised 1783) and Joshua (1799), as well as several daughters, and both his sons followed in his footsteps as joiners and remained in Headingley. It was his younger son, Joshua, who took over the farm after his father's death, as well as carrying on with joinery work. The elder son, John, had a joiner's workshop next to the Skyrack pub and took on general building work too, including at least one very ambitious project.[4]

Originally the way to the cottage and farm was across the village green to the side of the small school built by

Dean's Cottage, King's Place, seventeenth century – internal beams.

---

2. *Particulars and Valuation of the Estate of the Rt. Hon. James Earl of Cardigan, in the County of York, Surveyed and Valued by Jno. Bainbridge, 1792–8*, Northamptonshire Record Office, ASR 559. Copy on microfilm in Leeds Local Studies Library, MIC333.323C179.

3. Shown clearly as a separate property on the plan of allotments for sale under the Headingley-cum-Burley Enclosure Act, 1831 (WYAS Leeds, WYL160/M/350).

4. According to the inscription on the foundation stone of St Saviour's Church, Leeds, John Newland Hillas of Headingley was the builder of this impressive church (1842).

local subscription in 1783 (Samuel had been one of the subscribers). This was also the way to the public well next to the cottage, which was one of the water supplies for the village.[5] However, in 1831 what remained of the green was sold off as part of the sales which preceded the enclosure of all the remaining common land in Headingley. Once the land was sold a new road had to be provided to allow

5. Small boys could earn pocket money by filling people's water pots at the well for those without access to taps. (Memories of Headingley village, *Leeds Mercury*, 9.12.1931.)

Advertisement from 1905 for the carriages offered for hire by Spurdens, at St Michael's Livery Stables, converted from the outbuildings attached to the old cottage in St Michael's Lane.
(Leeds Library and Information Services)

TELEPHONE 0338.

SPURDENS,

St. Michael's Livery Stables,
St. Michael's Lane, Headingley.

FOR HIRE:
Rubber Tyred Broughams, Victorias, Landaus and Hansoms, Station Cabs, Large and Small   . . .
Waggonettes, Traps, etc.   .   .   .   .
Chars-a-banc for Private and Pic-nic Parties.

SPECIAL CLARENCE CARRIAGES FOR WEDDINGS
WITH BAY OR GREY HORSES.

Terms Reasonable.

RESIDENCE:

12, ASH ROAD,
NORTH LANE.

LEEDS   STATION   FARE   2s.
HEADINGLEY   STATION   FARE   1s.

access to the cottage and to the well. The 1834 Enclosure Award[6] designated two new roads: Well Road, now King's Place, which led to the well at the end (there is no trace of it now, though a small stream still runs through an adjoining garden, which presumably fed the well); and Hillas's Road, now Sagar Place, described as 'a private occupation road leading to an ancient enclosed Garth belonging to the Earl of Cardigan in the occupation of Joshua Hillas.' This became the only way to the cottage until St Michael's Lane was created 40 years later.[7]

Joshua Hillas continued to run the farm for many years, following in the footsteps of his predecessors. The Tithe Map of Headingley in 1846 shows that the shape and size of the farm had hardly changed since 1711: two of the same fields were in use, with another adjoining one. Next to the cottage there were stables, a cow house and a piggery. But all around the farm the environment was changing rapidly. On Headingley Moor, now divided up into fenced plots, and elsewhere in the village, spare land was being sold for villa development; the new Zoological and Botanical Gardens had opened nearby, bringing crowds of visitors; and the population was increasing rapidly as people moved out of the town to seek a more pleasant and healthy place to live. Joshua continued his carpentry work alongside the farm but was able to take advantage of the booming commercial life of the town; he offered lodgings in his house, and in 1841, when the census was taken, he had two foreign merchants, presumably with business in Leeds, lodging with him and his family.[8]

---

6. Enclosure Award and Map 1834 (WYAS Leeds, RDP39/162).

7. Sagar Place took its name from the Sagar family who owned the adjoining land and the large house, Spring House, which was built there, with an adjoining row of cottages, following the 1831 enclosure sale. It is now a cul-de-sac, with just a footpath through to the road behind. The stone house to one side, now called Muir Court, was already built by 1830 and probably dates back to the 1790s, when it belonged to John Cuttill, a fellmonger (deeds kindly lent to me by Robin Dove).

8. 1841 Census: H0107/1344/3/19.

The Hillases were evidently a well-respected village family. As tenants of Lord Cardigan they had a pew allocated to them when the new St Michael's Church was built in 1838. John Newland Hillas was elected more than once to be constable for the township in the 1830s. Their sons continued in the family joinery/building business until almost the end of the century, as 'master builders'. A stained-glass window dedicated to William Hillas (1804–1874), one of Samuel's grandsons, can still be seen in the present St Michael's Church.

But by the late 1860s the pace of change was quickening, and the existence of this small farm came under threat. The former Zoological and Botanical Gardens nearby were put up for sale for building development in 1869 and a new road, Cardigan Road, was formed to provide access and services. This cut right through the fields of the farm. Another new road, St Michael's Lane,[9] following close to the old farm boundary, was created to provide a cut-through to Cardigan Road from the village, bypassing the old narrow Chapel Lane and then continuing south by a narrow bridge across the railway, which had opened in 1849. The Cardigan trustees, keen after Lord Cardigan's death in 1868 to raise money to pay off the estate's massive debts, seized the opportunity and in the 1870s sold off the land between the cottage and Cardigan Road for villa development, breaking up the farm. Building began straight away and large semi-detached houses with long back gardens soon lined the northern side of Cardigan Road. Across the road, however, the fields remained, in spite of plans for new streets of high-density housing.[10]

---

9. Around this time the road leading from St Michael's Church down to the junction with North Lane and Cardigan Road, previously called Kirkstall Road and then Kirkstall Lane, was renamed St Michael's Road, as now. The 1881 Census still used the name Kirkstall Lane, but the OS map surveyed in 1889 had the new name of St Michael's Road.

10. The planned development is shown in a deed of 22.11.1872 in the John Goodchild collection, Wakefield. The plan was never put into effect.

At this stage the Hillas family gave up their tenancy of the cottage, after almost 100 years of occupancy. The cottage and what was left of the land was taken over by a new tenant, Michael Rayner, an Irishman, one of the new incomers taking advantage of the business opportunities this growing suburb could offer. He was a coal merchant, and he and his wife also ran a cab business, both useful services for the local residents. They continued to rent two fields across Cardigan Road, still undeveloped pasture land, presumably for grazing their horses, and they may well have continued to keep some cows and pigs as well. They took over the cab business which had been run from the Original Oak inn and for a while went on using the inn yard for their cabs.

In 1888, the Cardigan estate in Yorkshire was finally broken up and, in a huge four-day auction in Leeds, this small village property, among many others, was offered for sale, the cottage and the fields in separate lots. So the old farm which had been in existence for nearly 200 years, indeed very probably for much longer, finally disappeared. At the time of the sale, the cottage was described as having a sitting room, kitchen, dairy, and three bedrooms, with brick and slate outbuildings consisting of a coachhouse, four-stall stable, harness room, cow house for ten cows, and a piggery. Its origins as a farmhouse were still very evident. It was sold to the current tenant, Michael Rayner, for £455, and as part of the deal he had to pay £45 towards the cost of paving and kerbing St Michael's Lane, still a rough, unmade new road.

The fields across Cardigan Road which had been part of the farm were sold off separately as part of Lot 17a, which comprised over seventeen acres of 'beautifully timbered pasture and woodland... ripe for development', with frontages to Cardigan Road (830 feet) and Kirkstall Lane (550 feet). At the auction bids ran up to £11,000 but the lot was then withdrawn. This land was subsequently bought by a 'Company of Gentlemen' who formed the Leeds Cricket, Football and Athletic Company and in

1890 opened the Headingley Cricket and Rugby Grounds there: the beginning of another story.[11] Towards the end of the century the Company sold off its land fronting Cardigan Road as sites for villas, and the fields of the farm were gone for good, under bricks and gardens and the manicured turf of the cricket ground.

As for the cottage, now bereft of its land, it looks as though some time in the 1890s the 'business end' of the property, the coach house and stables etc., was separated off, and in 1899 various alterations were carried out to create a shop with living quarters above and stables behind.[12] By 1905 the business was advertised as St

Cottages in Cross Chapel Street. The cottages on the left were demolished in the early twentieth century. The one on the right, known as Ivy Cottage, is still there though now hemmed in by later buildings. *(Godfrey Bingley collection: reproduced with the permission of Leeds University Library)*

11. The initial purchasers were three Headingley residents, George Bray of Belmont, Wood Lane (see p.209), Charles F. Tetley of Spring Bank, Headingley Lane, and Frederick Barr of Mount View, solicitor. It is said that they scoured the Leeds directories for well-heeled backers to join the proposed company.

12. WYAS Leeds, Building Plans 1899/59.

Michael's Livery Stables, offering every kind of coach and carriage for hire as well as a cab service. During the First World War, as horses gave way to motor cars, the stables closed and after some years the property was converted into a garage (Pextons). In recent years the site became sadly neglected and derelict, but at the time of writing it has been cleared for development and building is in progress.

Meanwhile the old cottage survives, still lived in and enjoyed, as do a few others: Dean's Cottage in King's Place, which retains many of its original features; the house hidden away across the main road from the church, Ivy Lodge, also thought to be seventeenth century, originally a farmhouse and maybe an alehouse; Ivy Cottage in Cross Chapel Street, off North Lane, possibly equally ancient (a house is shown in roughly this position on the 1711 map); the property in Shire Oak Road once known as the

Cottages in St Michael's Road, opposite the Parish Centre, around 1900 (later demolished). One of these served as the village post office until c1890 – customers had to knock at a wooden shutter to be served. *(Thoresby Society)*

Old Farm, now the Yorkshire College of Music and Drama (see p.43). Many others survived until the close of the nineteenth century, only to be swept away in the course of the twentieth: a pair of old cottages in St Michael's Road; a small row in the main road near the corner of Wood Lane; others in North Lane, sacrificed to road widening and to the inevitable desire to modernise and update. In spite of this, and very surprisingly, the old farm buildings in Otley Road opposite Alma Road, once stables and a mistal (cowhouse), have survived some 200 years and are being preserved now (2008) within a new development. The traces of Headingley's old agricultural past are rare but not entirely lost.

Old cottages in Otley Road, on the corner of Wood Lane, photographed around 1895. Almost hidden behind the gigantic hoarding with its dizzying array of advertisements are three tiny stone cottages, with small gardens and a picket fence in front. These cottages were swept away around the end of the nineteenth century and replaced by purpose-built shops. *(Thoresby Society)*

Old farm buildings in the Otley Road opposite Shaw Lane in 2006, before development. This barn and mistal (cowhouse) date from the eighteenth century and stood in fields known as Far and Near Alder Close, part of a small farm. The fields were bought from the Cardigan estate in 1850 by William Boyne, a well-known antiquarian and numismatist, who had a large house called 'Woodlands' built on neighbouring land, set in extensive landscaped grounds. (The house was demolished when the Beckett Park estate was built in the 1930s.) Remarkably these old buildings survived different phases of use in the late nineteenth and twentieth centuries and at the time of writing are being incorporated into a new development on the site.

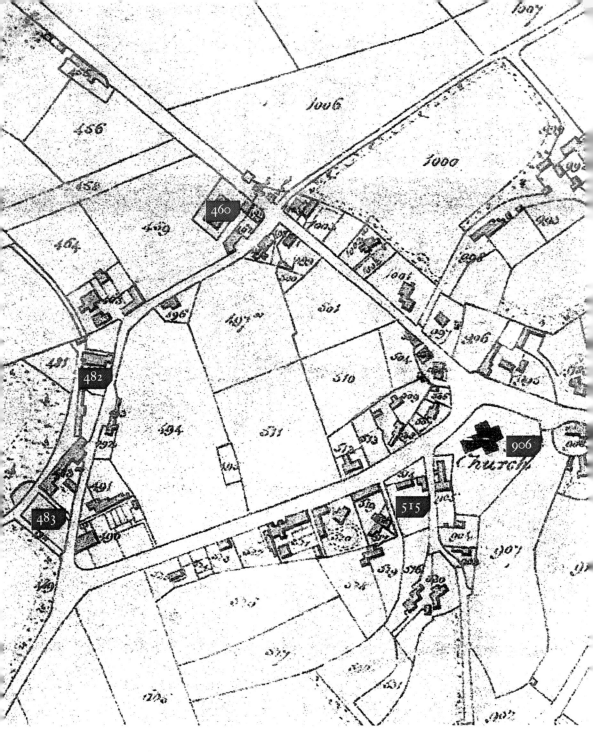

Detail of the village from the 1846 Tithe Map.

The growth of the village by 1846 can be seen on this map: a new larger church (906), a substantial Methodist chapel (460), the Town School and the master's house (515), and more buildings alongside the roads, built on former common land. A maltkiln (483) and tannery (482) can be seen in North Lane. The main road is now the Leeds-Otley Turnpike, with the tollbar and the tollkeeper's house shown near the junction with North Lane. There is a cluster of shops near the church and the pubs, in the heart of the village. Wood Lane is the only significant new road, designated as a footpath in 1834 following the Enclosure; otherwise the basic shape of the village remains much as it was in 1711. *(By permission of the National Archives, Kew)*

THE OTLEY ROAD

TOLLS AND TRAFFIC

IN THE HEART of the old village, where St Michael's Church looks across to the two pubs, the name of the main road changes from Headingley Lane to Otley Road, marked by the arrowed road sign on the wall of the Original Oak pub. The change reflects a major development some 250 years ago which had a considerable impact on village life.

At the start of the eighteenth century, the principal route from Leeds to Otley bypassed Headingley village. It went through Burley and then out along Spen Lane through Cookridge, and over the top of the Chevin steeply down to Otley,[1] following roughly the line we still call the 'Old Otley Road' (the 'new' road, the A660, did not exist then). It was an important and well-used route: the busy market town of Otley was a gateway to the cross Pennine routes into Lancashire and beyond into Scotland. The road which led from Leeds across the waste of Woodhouse Moor to Headingley was then just a narrow country lane leading to the village. However, the lane continued on through the village across Headingley Moor to Spen Lane,

---

1. This route was marked as 'the road from Otley to Leeds' on the 1711 Cardigan Estate Map.

where it joined the road to Cookridge and on to Otley, so it was an alternative route from the town.[2] The condition of all the roads was appalling: narrow and rocky, flooded after rain, slow and hazardous for packhorses and travellers and often impassable for carts and wagons.

PRESSURE FOR CHANGE

As traffic increased in the first half of the eighteenth century with the growth of trade, particularly in wool and cloth, the merchants of Leeds and other commercial centres saw an urgent need to improve their cross-country road connections. The only viable way to fund major road improvement particularly over long distances was through the turnpike system, already well tried elsewhere, whereby

---

2. It seems to have been a well-used alternative route from an early date. In the 1704 Quarter Sessions the Leeds magistrates ordered that the causeway on 'the highway' from Leeds to Otley through Headingley and across the Moor to Spen Lane should be repaired (WYAS Leeds, QL1/1); quoted by J.L.Cruickshank, op. cit.

Extract from the popular road book *A New and Accurate Description of all the Direct and Principal Cross Roads in England and Wales* by Daniel Paterson, 1794, showing Headingley on the route from London to Skipton via Leeds. *(Thoresby Society)*

LONDON to *Skipton*, by *Leeds*.

To *Leeds*, p. 149.		$192\frac{1}{2}$
Headingley	2	$194\frac{1}{2}$
Cookridge	$3\frac{1}{2}$	198
Otley	$4\frac{1}{2}$	$202\frac{1}{2}$
Burley	2	$204\frac{1}{2}$
Ilkley	4	$208\frac{1}{2}$
Addingham	3	$211\frac{1}{2}$
Skipton in Craven	6	$217\frac{1}{2}$

Other Roads, p. 148 *and* 153.

money could be borrowed from investors to pay for improvements in return for tolls paid by the road users.[3] The tolls were hated by those who had to pay them: in 1753 there had been riots at the toll bars at Pool, Harewood and Beeston, resulting in several deaths.[4] Nevertheless, in late 1754 a number of petitions, evidently well coordinated, were submitted to Parliament for the repair and improvement of the road from Leeds to Otley, from Otley to Skipton, and on into Lancashire, branching off to Colne, Burnley, Blackburn and Preston. This was an ambitious project requiring the establishment of a number

House and cottages in the Otley Road built around 1820 on the site of the old Toll Bar before it was moved nearer the junction with North Lane and Wood Lane. The bigger house on the left was the home and warehouse of Henry Charlesworth Windsor Mitchell, who ran his wine and spirit business there.

---

3. The old statutory system by which townships and parishes had a duty to maintain their own local roads could not cope with large-scale improvements across boundaries.

4. John Mayhall, *Annals of Yorkshire from the Earliest Period to the Present Time*, Leeds, 1866: entry for June 1753.

of turnpike trusts, each responsible for a particular section of the road. It had support from merchants in all the major centres of trade, particularly the weaving areas, as well as from some (but not all) local landowners. Supporting evidence from a series of witnesses was presented to the parliamentary committee set up to consider the petitions. Henry Hitch, a Leeds merchant and Receiver of Land Tax for the West Riding, attested that the road from Leeds to Otley, which he knew well, was 'much frequented' but was in very bad condition, narrow, quite impassable for carriages in winter, and impossible to keep in repair. Sir Henry Ibbetson, one of the Leeds 'gentlemen merchants', gave evidence of the benefits to trade, particularly for Leeds, which would result from improvements to the road between Leeds and Otley and beyond into the weaving areas.[5] Consent was given for a Bill, and the Act received royal assent in June 1755.[6]

A trust was set up for the Leeds to Otley section of the road – the Leeds-Otley Turnpike Trust. The trustees lost no time in advertising for investors willing to put money into the project in return for 4% interest, but it looks as though it was some time before enough money was forthcoming, as three years were to pass before they advertised for tenders for the making of the road.[7] Bids may have been slow to come in, as the notice had to be repeated several times and the deadline extended. However, the project finally got under way and the decision was taken to construct the first part of the route, from Leeds out to Spen Lane, through Headingley village rather than along the old line of the road through Burley: the route through Headingley was rather more direct and

5. Journals of the House of Commons, 28.1.1755. Sir Henry Ibbetson also claimed that estates along the road would double in value as a result of the improved road. The evidence to the committee was well coordinated: a meeting of all interested parties had been called beforehand to make the necessary arrangements: public notice in the *Leeds Intelligencer*, 30.12.1754.

6. 28 George II cap.60.

7. Notices in the *Leeds Intelligencer*, 1.7.1755 and 28.11.1758.

A tollbar ticket for Headingley Bar, which, after payment, ensured free passage at the Woodhouse and Spen Lane bars and a reduction at certain other bars. Printed tickets were introduced in 1821, and each bar had its own distinctive ticket colour. *(West Yorkshire Archive Service, Wakefield)*

less hilly. By 1770, when Thomas Jefferys drew up his map of Yorkshire, the new Leeds to Otley turnpike road was shown running through Headingley village, as it does now, then out to Spen Lane, on to Cookridge, and over the Chevin to Otley. By 1794 Headingley figured in one of the most popular road books of the time as a named place on the London to Skipton route via Leeds. With the improved turnpike road came increased traffic, better links with the town of Leeds and centres elsewhere, and an opening up of village life – an incidental effect of this major commercial development.

GATES AND TOLLS

The 1755 Act empowered the Trust to erect tollgates (turnpikes) and set out a complex table of tolls to be charged for horses, coaches and carriages (according to the number of horses), wagons and carts, and for droves of cattle, pigs, sheep etc. People on foot (the majority of ordinary folk) went through free of charge. A man on a horse paid 1d.; a coach drawn by six horses paid 1s. 6d.;

LEEDS AND OTLEY TURNPIKE ROAD.

SCALE of TOLLS, commencing July 1st, 1845.

Description of Carriage and Wheels.	1st BAR.		2nd BAR.	
	s.	d.	s.	d.
For every Horse or Beast drawing any Coach, Berlin, Chariot, Post-Chaise, Calash, Phaeton, Hearse, Litter, Chaise, Chair, Gig, or any such like Carriage, the Sum of	0 ,, 8		0 ,, 4	
For every Horse or Beast of Draught, drawing any Stage-Coach, Diligence, Van, Caravan, Stage-Waggon, or other Stage-Carriage or Cart, usually employed in carrying Passengers or Goods for pay or reward, the Sum of	0 ,, 5		0 ,, 5	
For every Horse or Beast of Draught, drawing any Waggon, Wain, Van, Cart, or such like Carriage, laden or unladen, having the Fellies of the Wheels thereof of the breadth of Six Inches or upwards, the Sum of	0 ,, 5½		0 ,, 3	
And having the Fellies of the Wheels thereof of the breadth of Four Inches and a Half, and less than Six Inches, the Sum of	0 ,, 6½		0 ,, 3¼	
And having the Fellies of the Wheels thereof of less breadth than Four Inches and a Half, the Sum of	0 ,, 8		0 ,, 4	
And having the Fellies of the Wheels thereof of the breadth of Four Inches and a Half or upwards, with perfectly flat tire and no projecting nails, and running flat on the whole breadth of the tire, the Sum of	0 ,, 4		0 ,, 3	
For every Four-Wheeled Carriage of any description, which shall be fastened, or in any manner fixed, to another Carriage, the Sum of	1 ,, 0		0 ,, 6	
And for every Two-Wheeled Carriage so fastened and fixed, the Sum of	0 ,, 8		0 ,, 4	
For every Horse, Mule, or Ass, laden or unladen, and not drawing, the Sum of	0 ,, 2		0 ,, 2	
For every Drove of Oxen or Neat Cattle per Score, and so in proportion for any greater or less number, the Sum of ..	0 ,, 10		0 ,, 10	
For every Drove of Calves, Swine, Sheep or Lambs, per Score, and so in proportion for any greater or less number, the Sum of	0 ,, 5		0 ,, 5	
For every Carriage moved or propelled by Steam or Machinery, or by any other Power than Animal Power, the Sum of ..	3 ,, 0		3 ,, 0	

In all cases where there shall be a fractional part of a Half-penny in the calculation or amount of the said Tolls, the Sum of One Half-penny shall be demanded and taken in lieu of such fractional part.

The Tolls payable for Horses or Beasts of Draught drawing any Stage-Coach, Diligence, Van, Caravan, Stage-Waggon, or other Stage-Carriage, or Cart, and also for any Carriage moved or propelled by Steam or Machinery, or by any other Power than Animal Power, conveying Passengers or Goods for pay or reward, are payable every time of passing or repassing along the

The scale of tolls on the Leeds and Otley Turnpike Road introduced in 1845. The width of wheels was a factor in the charges, as narrow wheels were known to damage the surface of the roads more than broader ones: the narrower the wheels the higher the toll. The advent of new technology was recognised: vehicles powered by steam or machinery or 'any other Power than Animal Power' were now covered, but were subject to a high charge. *(West Yorkshire Archive Service, Wakefield)*

a coach drawn by a single horse 4d.; a wagon drawn by four horses or oxen 1s.; a drove of cattle 5d. a score. There were exemptions for carts carrying various goods: coal and fuel, manure and other farming necessities, building materials, cloth for the fulling mills, corn for the corn mills. There was no charge for people going to church or attending funerals or parliamentary elections, and for soldiers on the march. Two toll gates were set up initially, in Woodhouse Lane and at Otley. The trustees farmed out the business of collecting the tolls in return for the payment of rent, a common system which was later blamed for many of the problems which beset the Trust. When the tolls on the Leeds-Otley road were advertised for letting in 1774[8] the profit in the previous year was said to be £450, a fairly substantial sum. The businessmen who took the job on were of course more interested in protecting their profits than in keeping the road well maintained. While the townships through which the road passed had a statutory duty to provide labour and materials for road maintenance, the cost was resented by local ratepayers and the standard of work was often shoddy. Meanwhile the investors who had put up the cash originally wanted a return on their money, putting pressure on the Trust's finances.

The Trust, like many others, soon found itself in debt. In 1781, 1802 and 1821 the trustees applied for further Acts of Parliament to enable them to borrow more money to fund further road repairs and improvements.[9] Changes in the rates of tolls were authorised and a minimum width set for the wheels of vehicles using the roads, as it was recognised that narrow wheels had a ruinous effect on the road surface, which was just broken stones laid on top of earth, soon rutted, muddy and pot-holed. The extra funding enabled some improvements to be carried out: in particular, in the early 1800s, a new straighter section of road was built past Weetwood Hall (on the current line of the road) to join the old road at Lawnswood, so avoiding the narrow curves of Spen Lane.

The 1821 Act, which consolidated previous legislation, put the management of the road more firmly under the direct control of the trustees, who included several prominent Headingley men, among them Thomas Bischoff, John Marshall and Christopher Beckett. The Act introduced a number of new features: proper records to be kept; printed tickets to be issued at the bars; standards for weighing machines to check the weight of carts and their loads; exemptions for mail coaches; more toll bars to be set up along the route but with waivers if people had already

8. *Leeds Mercury*, 1.2.1774.
9. 21 George III cap.98; 42 George III cap.15; 1 George IV cap.94.

paid at the previous bar; power for the toll keeper to impound stray cattle; and new and improved toll houses, with gardens and lamps (essential on dark nights).[10] Penalties were set for various misdemeanours, including playing football on the road, letting off fireworks, letting pigs root up the road surface, and butchering animals so that blood ran onto the road (a hefty fine of £5 for all of these). A highway code was established, with riders and vehicles having to keep to the left of the road, and it was expressly forbidden to leave a coach or wagon blocking the road (parking problems are nothing new).

A New Tollhouse in Headingley

Some time after 1775 land was bought by the trustees for the erection of a third tollhouse and turnpike gate on the route, located just beyond Headingley village, opposite what is now Alma Road and next to the old farm outbuildings which still survive there. It looks as though this tollhouse was replaced by a new one in 1803, and the 'old tollhouse' as it was called was sold off. It was later demolished and around 1820 a row of cottages was built on the site, which are still there and in use.[11] In 1821 the Turnpike Road trustees chose a new site for the Headingley tollhouse: they went to view some 'waste land near the North Lane End' and decided that they would build there;[12] meanwhile, a chain was put across the road and a temporary hut erected for the tollkeeper. A sketch plan of 1854 shows the tollhouse on the corner opposite

10. From 1821 onwards, records of the Leeds-Otley Turnpike Trust survive and are held by the WYAS, Wakefield, in three boxes, ref. RT61. These records are the source of much of the information on the Trust included here. See also W.F. Seals, *Notes on the Leeds and Otley Turnpike Road 1821–1873*, 1958 (Leeds Local Studies Library LQP352.62 SE15), and C. Campbell, *A Study of the Development of the Turnpike Road system around the town of Otley, 1750–1890*, 1978 (Otley Museum dc/3).

11. WYAS Leeds, Deeds, Acc. 1151.

12. WYAS Wakefield, Records of the Leeds and Otley Turnpike Road, RT61, Minute Book.

North Lane (where the Arndale Centre is now) projecting out into the road, with its gate and the cattle pound (the pinfold) nearby where the tollkeeper could shut up any stray animals wandering through the gate; the owner would have to pay 10s. plus expenses to get them out again. This tollhouse was to remain in use for some 50 years.

Further improvements to the road were carried out in 1830 when the section between Woodhouse Moor and Headingley village was straightened and widened, and a high causeway (pavement) provided on the north side to keep people on foot out of the mud and safe from passing vehicles. The improvement of the road eased commuting into town, a benefit for the increasing number of well-to-do merchants moving to Headingley to escape the worsening living conditions of Leeds while being close enough for daily travel to town. It also opened the way for further development: for new housing on Headingley Moor following the 1834 enclosure, and for the forthcoming attraction of the Zoological and Botanical Gardens, which opened in 1840.

A New Route

For travellers on longer journeys and most particularly for the important and lucrative commercial traffic the main problem with the road over the Chevin remained the terrible steepness of the descent to Otley and the ascent on the way to Leeds. The gradient put a severe strain on the horses pulling heavy loads and was terrifying for riders and passengers. It was usual for coach passengers to get out at the top of the Chevin and walk down rather than face the dangers of an accident in the coach, and people often walked on the way up too to ease the burden on the straining horses.[13] For the road to stay competitive in the face of alternative routes and the challenge of the newly developing railway network it became essential to find a better route.

---

13. Fred Cobley, *On Foot through Wharfedale*, Otley, 1882.

In 1836 the trustees decided to employ George Hayward of Headingley Hall, the land surveyor who acted as Lord Cardigan's agent in Yorkshire, to determine the best line for the road in order to avoid the Chevin. He advised on a route along the side of the hill below Bramhope village, more or less the line which the current road (the A660) follows. It was decided to go ahead on this basis, a project which the trustees promoted as of 'great public utility', and application was made for an enabling Act of Parliament. Again there were objections: the Leeds Surveyors of the Highways claimed that the new road was not needed and various landowners objected to it crossing their land. But the Act was passed in June 1837, 'to afford a more convenient and commodious communication between the Town of Leeds and the Towns of Otley, Ilkley etc… by avoiding a very steep hill called The Chivin'.[14] George Hayward was appointed as surveyor to supervise the work of excavating and constructing the new road: it proved difficult and demanding. The first contractor went bankrupt and another had to be employed. The road took five years to build, but finally opened in 1842.

---

14. 7 William IV cap.36.

One of the milestones erected on the new route of the Leeds-Otley Turnpike, opened in 1842, which bypassed the steep ascent and descent of the Chevin on the old road. The Turnpike Trust was required to set up milestones at key places along the route. This one stands in Bramhope.

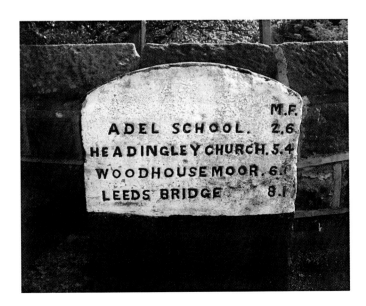

The cost was crippling. The work had gone £5,000 over estimate and the Trust's debts rose in these few years from under £2,000 to over £20,000. And that was not the end of it, as there were constant problems with the maintenance of the new road, particularly at Pool Bank where quarry landslips caused endless difficulties, resulting finally in legal action. The whole road was in need of investment, but the Trust had no money for the necessary repairs: the rents from letting the tolls were too low and interest had to be paid on the mountainous debts. In Headingley there were particular problems over the stone needed for surfacing the road. This had always been taken free of charge from the quarry on Headingley Moor, as indeed had stone for the township roads in Leeds, but after the Moor was enclosed in 1834 this was no longer allowed. Workmen trying to collect stone were marched off in handcuffs by the village constable to face the magistrates. Legal opinion was taken but the advice was that stone from the quarry now had to be paid for.

Within a short time the road was in a terrible state and the desperate trustees abandoned the task of repair, leaving it to the local townships to do what they could with their section of the road. In return they were taken to court. In 1845 the road expert Richard Bayldon was called in to report and declared the road to be 'soft, muddy, and indeed extremely dangerous'.[15] Bayldon took on the post of surveyor to the road; he condemned the system of letting out the tolls as a 'criminal mode of doing business' and introduced various measures to improve the management of the tolls and the maintenance work, as well as setting new scales of tolls and organising additional bars, at Hyde Park (a chain), Spen Lane (another chain), and further out, at Bramhope and Pool Bank (where the tollhouse can still be seen). Slowly the condition of the road improved,

15. WYAS Wakefield: Records of the Leeds and Otley Turnpike Road, RT 61 Box 1; Report to the trustees by Richard Bayldon, 1845. Richard Bayldon was appointed surveyor to several Turnpike Trusts, was the author of several pamphlets on road management, and in 1857 published a book on *Road Legislation and Management*.

though in 1851 the surface was still reported as poor or very bad in most parts. Headingley was luckier, as the surface there was said to be tolerable though rough; perhaps it helped that some of the trustees lived there. There was further improvement in 1853 when the trustees embarked on new technology and had parts of the road 'macadamised', surfaced with small evenly sized stones which were compacted with a 'roller' to form a harder, more robust surface.[16]

Competition from the ever-growing railway network was a fear, and in 1845 loomed nearer as the foundation stone was laid for the Leeds-Thirsk railway which was to serve Burley and Headingley and connect them with Leeds and with the towns to the north. However, the railway was forced by the intransigence of local landowners to take a line well to the south of Headingley village, which meant it was not so convenient for residents in the well-to-do areas around the village. After encountering massive problems in the construction of the Bramhope tunnel, the new line finally opened in 1849, but, given the position of the station, it seems not to have offered a major challenge to the road at least for local commuting traffic.

The Trust's debts were slowly reduced, but there seemed no prospect of being able to pay them off. The trustees offered a settlement to their mortgagees but this was not accepted, so they took legal opinion. They were firmly advised that the money they got from the tolls should be spent on maintaining the road and not finish up in the pockets of the mortgagees – anything else would be 'a monstrous injustice'. The users of the road were in any case not happy with the level of tolls they had to pay, and in 1862 a number of Headingley residents made a formal complaint that the tolls were too high for travelling such a short distance into town. They did achieve a reduction. Others found ways of avoiding the tolls, a practice sternly forbidden in the legislation. In one case the trustees took

---

16. Not to be confused with 'tarmacadam', a much later, separate development.

an enterprising businessman to court for riding up to the gate in a cab, walking through free of charge to conduct his affairs, then returning to the cab, but they lost the case.[17] Another way of avoiding paying was to use the smaller byroads. However, this was not always welcomed by other residents: in 1865 the wealthy residents of Oil Mill Lane (now Wood Lane) published a statement that it was a private road with no right of access for the public and they intended to put a chain across it to stop people using it.[18]

---

17. The Magistrates declared he had done nothing wrong, much to the trustees' annoyance. WYAS Wakefield, RT61 Box 3.

18. Over a century later, similar (though differently motivated) action was taken by the Council to bar through-traffic from Wood Lane, a move which has happily preserved its peaceful atmosphere.

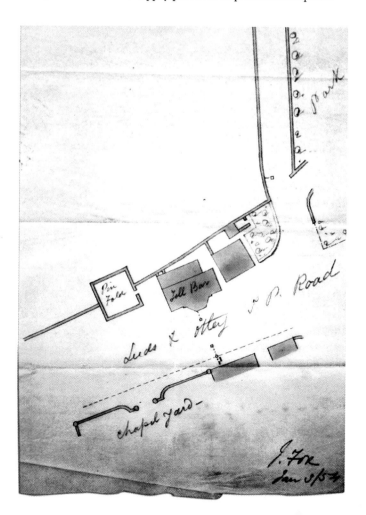

The Toll Bar in Headingley, just beyond the junction with Wood Lane and North Lane, in a sketch plan dated 1854. The tollkeeper lived in the Bar house. The pinfold is shown next to the Bar, where the tollkeeper could shut up any animal straying through the gate. The owner had to pay a fee to reclaim it. *(West Yorkshire Archive Service, Leeds)*

LEEDS AND HEADINGLEY OMNIBUS.—

JOHN WOOD, Proprietor of the ORIGINAL LEEDS and HEADINGLEY OMNIBUS, is anxious to express his grateful Acknowledgments for the Patronage bestowed upon this Conveyance from its Establishment in June, 1838, and since Novr., 1839, when the kindness of his Friends enabled him to take the entire responsibility and interest into his own Hands.

J. W. has had his Omnibus thoroughly repaired and renovated during the last few Weeks, and has it now upon the Road again. From and after Monday next, he will perform one extra Journey each Day; namely, from Headingley at Half-past Six, and from Leeds at Seven o'Clock in the Evening. The Times of Departure, therefore, will be as follows :—

From Mr. ASKEY'S Three Horse-Shoes, Far Headingley,	From Mrs. CLARKE'S, Oak Inn, Headingley.	From Mrs. SUTCLIFFE'S, Wheat Sheaf Inn, Upperhead-Row, Leeds.
25 Minutes to Nine	Quarter to Nine	Half-past Nine
20 Min. past Ten	Half-past Ten	One
20 Min. past Two	Half-past Two	Three
10 Min. to Five	Five	Half-past Five
20 Min. past Six	Half-past Six	Seven
10 Min. to Eight	Eight	Half-past Eight.

For the Accommodation of the Residents and Visiters of MEANWOOD, J. W. will extend Two Journeys each Day to the BECKETT'S ARMS, to and from whence the Times of Departure will be :—

From LEEDS to MEANWOOD : Half-past Nine Morning.
Ditto······Ditto········Seven Evening.
From MEANWOOD to LEEDS : Ten Minutes past Ten Morning.
Ditto······Ditto····Twenty Minutes to Eight Evening

ON SUNDAYS :—

From MEANWOOD.	THREE HORSE SHOES, HEADINGLEY.	LEEDS.
Morning··Half-past Nine	Quarter to Ten	Quarter to One.
Evening···················	20 Min. past Five	Six.
10 Min. past Seven	20 Min. past Seven	Eight.

JOHN WOOD is LICENSED to LET POST HORSES, and has provided a NEW and COMMODIOUS COACH, for Extra Service and occasional Parties.

PARCELS PUNCTUALLY AND CAREFULLY DELIVERED.
Far-Headingley, 23rd Sept., 1841.

Advertisement in the Leeds Mercury on 2 October 1841 for John Wood's restored horse-drawn omnibus service between Far Headingley and Leeds, initiated in 1838. He now offered six journeys a day, together with a new twice-daily service to and from Meanwood.

By the mid-1860s the Trust, like many others, was still deeply in debt, though the income from tolls remained fairly healthy. This was not the case on many other turnpike roads, where competition from the railways meant diminishing tolls, and there was much pressure for change. In 1866 the Leeds Improvement Act enabled the Corporation to take over the turnpike roads and abolish the hated tolls. The Corporation acted quickly to implement its new powers and began the purchase of all the turnpike roads and the removal of the toll bars, amid much jubilation. When the bar at Woodhouse Moor was due to be abolished, at midnight on 31 January 1867, a specially hired bus and various cabs full of Headingley residents arrived and on the stroke of midnight passed through the opened gate singing and playing a variety of noisy musical instruments in celebration.[19] While some of the Trust's tollhouses were sold off, the Headingley tollhouse, inconveniently protruding into the highway, was demolished and the site used to widen the road.

Traffic

What of the traffic which made its way through Headingley along the turnpike road? In the early years, the traffic was mainly commercial, the heavy wagons and carts of the carriers, packhorses with their loads of goods, and droves of animals being taken to market, together with local farm carts and some private traffic – the carriages, gigs and horses of the well-to-do. By the end of the eighteenth century, there was a regular mail service, taken by messenger every morning from Leeds to Otley and back in the evening,[20] and stage coaches had begun to use the route. In 1807 a regular coach, the Union, started running three times a week from Leeds to Kendal, changing horses at Otley; it left Leeds at six in the

---

19. *Leeds Mercury*, 2.2.1867.

20. *Holden's Triennial Directory*, 1805–7.

morning and returned at five the next morning, and later became a daily service until its closure in 1843. In 1816 it was joined by the True Briton on the same route, three times a week, and in 1822 another coach, the Defiance, began to run three times a week from Ilkley to Leeds, returning the same day.[21] The fare was 4s. inside and 2s. 6d. outside, which were high charges beyond many people's means: they could travel more cheaply if they could find a place in one of the carriers' wagons which travelled daily between Leeds and Otley, laden with goods. In the 1840s competition from the railways brought an end to the stage coach services, but by then a new form of transport had made its appearance in Headingley.[22]

As more businessmen in Leeds chose to move out to new residences in or near Headingley to escape the smoke and pollution, they had the problem of daily travel into town. Buying a horse and carriage or hiring a cab was expensive. So in 1838 a group of Headingley residents got together to form a company to fund a horse-drawn omnibus between the village and the town on a regular basis. The service was instituted on 25 June 1838, just three days before the coronation of Queen Victoria. It was the first suburban bus service in Leeds (Headingley still has the number 1 bus) and was to set the model for many others. 'A very neat omnibus has commenced running from Headingley to Leeds for the accommodation of merchants and others. The fare is only 6d.' reported the *Leeds Mercury* on 30 June 1838. The bus ran five journeys daily out to the Three Horseshoes Inn at Far Headingley, serving residents in the newly developing area beyond the

---

21. Tom Bradley, *The Old Coaching days in Yorkshire*, Otley, 1889.

22. For full information on nineteenth century public transport in Leeds see J. Soper, *Leeds Transport, Vol. I, 1830–1902*, published by the Leeds Transport Historical Society, 1985. This series of publications, brought up to modern times in later volumes, is an extremely valuable and comprehensive source of information on the development of road transport in Leeds and its suburbs. I am most grateful to the Society for permission to use material from their publications in this chapter.

village as well. The bus was operated by John Wood, who lived in Headingley, and it was clearly a successful venture as by 1839 he was able to pay off his debts to the company of residents and complete payment for the bus.

In the following year, 1840, the new Zoological and Botanical Gardens opened in Headingley, and created a sudden surge in demand. John Wood struggled to keep going but had to take his bus off the road for a month in 1841 for repair and renovation. When it returned to service he put on an extra journey, making six daily, and he later increased this to seven, but by now there was competition on the route and he finally went bankrupt. Two larger firms took over and from 1845 Headingley enjoyed a service of twelve horse-drawn buses each day, running approximately hourly between 9 am and 8.30 pm. The buses had to pay a compound charge for passage along the turnpike road, which meant the fare remained high; in 1851 the bus

A horse bus on the Headingley route. In the early years people complained about the cramped and sometimes dirty conditions, and the disturbance caused by the conductor blowing his horn as the bus approached. *(Thoresby Society)*

owners made a formal objection to the turnpike Trust[23] and achieved a reduction. However, the fare was still beyond the means of the ordinary working man and the timing wrong: this was a service for the middle-class professional men commuting to town.

Welcome as the service was initially, the buses were the cause of many complaints. Some were single decker, holding six to twelve people in a small space, perhaps six foot by four, while others had seats on top, open to the elements and hence unpopular. The buses were often old, cramped and dirty, forcing people into unwelcome close contact with their fellow travellers. The conductor was likely to be a grubby small boy who as well as taking the fares blew loudly on his horn to signal the bus's approach, disturbing local residents. There were plenty of letters to the press, voicing dissatisfaction with these 'Headingley inconveniences'.

The Trams

The later years of the century saw rapid changes in the traffic along the road, as new inventions and technologies were tried out. The development of these faster, cheaper, more frequent commuting services undoubtedly contributed to the rapid growth of Headingley as a residential suburb not just for the well-to-do but for ordinary working people too. In 1871 the popular and profitable Headingley route was chosen for the first horse-drawn tramway in Leeds, promoted by a private company which later became the Leeds Tramway Company. Construction of the grooved metal track began in June 1871, was completed to the Original Oak inn by early September, and then continued out to the Three Horseshoes, where tram sheds were later constructed to house the trams at the end of the line.[24] The carriages were bigger than the buses and could be pulled

---

23. *Leeds Mercury*, 24.5.1851.

24. Much later converted to a bus garage; demolished in the 1990s to make way for apartments.

along the track by only two or three horses, though on steep inclines such as Cookridge Street an additional 'chain' horse was needed. The trams carried more passengers than the buses and so a cheaper, more frequent service could be provided: just 3d. to the Oak inn. There were still no fixed stops: people simply put up their hand to get on, and could be dropped off wherever they wanted. But the trams were not welcomed by horse-owners. In December 1871 Arthur Lupton of Headingley Castle submitted a claim for damages to his carriage from track which stuck up above the road level, and a number of other accidents to horses and carriages were reported. Nevertheless in March 1874 the Company Chairman was able to claim that the Headingley tramway was 'the best piece of tramway in the kingdom.'

However, there were problems, and concern that the heavy double-decker tramcars were cruelly hard for the horses to haul. So the Company experimented with yet

A horse tram, drawn by three horses, in Otley Road. The horse trams, running along metal tracks, were introduced in 1871. The trams had larger carriages then the buses and so could take more passengers. This photograph dates from the 1890s. *(Godfrey Bingley collection: reproduced with the permission of Leeds University Library)*

another new invention: steam traction, replacing the horses by a steam engine to pull the cars along the tramway. In 1883, after the track had been relaid, steam tramcars were introduced on the Headingley route. The engines were built at the Monkbridge Ironworks, owned by James Kitson, later Lord Airedale;[25] from Spring Bank, his mansion in Headingley Lane, he must have been able to watch his great engines wheezing their way past. But local residents were not happy. The newspapers were flooded with complaints about 'this diabolical machine' sending out 'one continuous stream of sparks ten or twelve feet high and covering passengers on the top with pieces of cinder';[26]

A steam tram on the Headingley route in the 1890s. The steam trams were introduced in 1883. The powerful steam engines could easily pull the heavy tram carriages, relieving the horses of this arduous work, but they were dirty and noisy and the subject of much complaint. *(Godfrey Bingley collection: reproduced with the permission of Leeds University Library)*

25. James Kitson (1835–1911), son of the founder of the great Kitson engineering empire, a prominent Liberal and friend of Gladstone, Mayor of Leeds in 1896, Lord Mayor in 1897. He moved from Spring Bank to Gledhow Hall in 1885. He was created first Baron Airedale in 1907.

26. *Yorkshire Post*, 18.1.1883.

the engines frightened horses and riders and made walking unbearable because of the 'sickening fumes' they gave off. When they took in water from the hydrant at the Original Oak they discharged great gusts of steam, another cause for much complaint. But in spite of all the protests these moving monsters continued to run and made cheaper travel possible, so that by 1888 the maximum fare any-where was 2d., and services were even more frequent. However, there were increasing problems with the track and in 1891 it was reported that some Headingley ratepayers were considering taking legal action; urgent repair work had to be undertaken, with resulting chaos for travellers.

As the century drew to a close, horse buses, horse trams and steam trams all served the residents of Headingley in their journeys to and from town. Other forms of private transport had already appeared: in 1869 the *Mercury* reported an accident in Headingley when a horse drawing a wagonette bolted at the terrifying sight of a group of velocipedists on the road.[27] But private transport was still primarily by horse: in later memories, the village was said to be 'thronged with coaches and pairs'. All the wealthy local residents had their own carriages and horses, like Alf Cook the printing tycoon who lived at Weetwood Hall and had 'his own private hansom, all polished brass fittings, and a coachman with a cockade'.[28] The horse was still king of the road. But change was looming, both for public and private transport.

When the Tramways Company was taken over by the Corporation in 1894 the vexed question of traction had to be tackled. Horses were slow, steam engines useful but unpleasant, and there was now a new option, electric power, already in use on the route to Roundhay Park.

27. *Leeds Mercury*, 19.6.1869. The velocipede was a forerunner of the bicycle.

28. *Leeds Evening News*, articles on memories of old Headingley, 9.11.1955 and 10.11.1955.

Meanwhile, in June 1895 complaints were made at a City Council meeting about the Headingley service: people at the outer end of the route could not get back from town because of overcrowding and this was affecting the letting of property. It was claimed that Headingley businessmen were moving out to Harrogate and Ilkley because it was quicker to reach home by train from Leeds than to get a horse tram back to Headingley. More buses were put on and more horses bought but it was clear that another solution was needed.

A decision was finally made in favour of electrification of the tram system and work on the Headingley route began in 1899. The landscape changed as the tall, rather decorative poles which carried the overhead wires were erected along the route, and in the village the stone wall which ran along the road by the Shire Oak tree had to be moved back to make room, leaving the tree islanded within a railed enclosure. In June and July that year special electric cars were run to Headingley from City Square for people attending the Test Match, and on 3 January 1900 a regular passenger service was brought into operation, with frequent trams running from early morning to late evening at a reduced fare. 'A revolution in the lives of the inhabitants' was the claim. In 1899 the final horse bus running to Headingley was withdrawn and within two more years the horse trams also disappeared from the scene. The electric trams were to run through Headingley until the late 1950s when the internal combustion engine won the day.

A surviving horse trough, Otley Road – no horses drink from it now. (Maker, R. Asquith & Co, Meanwood Road Foundry, c.1875.)

And Then...

It was around the turn of the century too that the first motor cars appeared on the road. Ernest Beckett, who lived at Kirkstall Grange (Beckett Park) was the proud owner of a 'Gladiator' car, which was used in 1902 to drive Rowland Winn, the first motor car agent in Leeds (later Lord Mayor and a Headingley resident), to his wedding, billed in the papers as the first motor car wedding in Leeds. In 1906 a special motor bus service was introduced to take people from the Far Headingley tram terminus out to the newly developing suburb of Adel. This was very useful for golfers belonging to Headingley golf club, which had just moved from Spen Lane to Adel; as the transport company directors were golfers, there were inevitable accusations of favouritism. More motor buses made their appearance in Headingley rather later, initially as an addition to the tram service and serving the new outer suburbs. Although at first unpopular, unreliable, smelly and noisy, motor transport quickly took over, especially after the First World War. Stables were converted into garages, coachmen became chauffeurs. Today, along the road to Otley just one of the once numerous horse troughs survives opposite the end of Burton Crescent, a battered relic of the age of the horse.[29]

During the twentieth century the Otley Road (now the A660) did not escape its troubled past. As traffic increased to the point of saturation, it became the subject of deep division over its future. From the 1930s until the 1980s a number of abortive schemes were proposed for a bypass, involving road-widening, demolition of old buildings, even at one time the construction of a 'spaghetti junction' at the Shaw Lane crossroads. All of these were defeated by campaigns of public protest. They were followed by

29. Horses were not trouble-free. The Council's Street and Scavenging Department had a duty to clear the roads regularly of horse droppings (then sold as manure to farmers and gardeners) – *Leeds Sanitary Committee Reports, 1883–1913.*

proposals for a new high-speed tram route running behind the Arndale Centre, but this too has finally(?) been abandoned. So the village centre of Headingley remains much as it was. While the road through is at times choked with buses, vans and cars and is always difficult and dangerous to cross – still 'much frequented' as was claimed in 1754, though by traffic of a kind unimaginable when those words were written – it has kept its shape and its human dimension, a measure of continuity for which we can perhaps be thankful.

THE PUBS

THE ORIGINAL OAK AND THE SKYRACK

THE TWO PUBS in the centre of Headingley village, the Original Oak and the Skyrack, have faced each other across the road for over 200 years, rivals for customers in search of refreshment.

The Original Oak

The Original Oak is almost certainly the older. It was definitely in business as an alehouse in 1798, and it may well have been a hostelry long before that.[1] In origin it was a farmhouse, with a garden, an adjoining small enclosure of land, and fields outside the village. The property was owned by Lord Cardigan like most of the village, but was rented out on a series of 21 year leases as was customary with the small farms on the Cardigan estate. There was a house on this site in 1711, shown on the first map of the village, and the tenant at the time was Robert Carrett, who

---

1. It has been suggested that it can be identified as the inn in Headingley listed in military records in 1686, and that it may have served the drovers bringing cattle and other animals down from Scotland to market in Leeds. If so, the fields associated with the house may have provided overnight grazing for the drovers' livestock. See J.L.Cruickshank, *Headingley-cum-Burley c1540–c1784*, PhD Thesis (unpublished), University of Leeds, 2003.

came from a long-established Headingley family.[2] He rented the house, garden and adjoining land together with two fields along Kirkstall Lane called Far Leaker and Near Leaker. The house was in a good position for an alehouse, and the routing of the turnpike road from Leeds to Otley through the village in 1755 must have meant plenty of passing trade. The original house may have been extended or rebuilt around then, as in 1781, when it appears on John Tuke's map of Leeds, it is shown more or less in its present position, next to the road. Alongside the inn, the landlord continued to run the associated smallholding, which remained virtually unchanged for the next hundred years or more. In the early 1800s, the same fields that Robert Carrett had rented in 1711 were still being rented by the inn's current landlord, also called Robert Carrett and presumably a descendant, a pattern of continuity not yet disturbed by the changes the new century would bring. He had another business too, selling stone from the quarry on Headingley Moor which he rented from the Cardigan estate – in 1806 he got into trouble with the village constable and the local manorial court for not fencing the quarry, 'to the great danger of the cattle pasturing on the Moor'.[3] When he died in 1814, 'much respected' as his gravestone in St Michael's churchyard records, his widow Jane carried on running the inn.

The inn was known originally as 'The Oak' or sometimes 'The Oak Tree' or 'The Skyrack Oak'. It was listed as 'The Oak Tree' in Baines's Directory of 1817,[4] the first directory to include inns in the villages outside the town. The name derived of course from the famous oak tree known as the Shire Oak, or Skyrack, which stood close by. When Joseph Clark and his wife Hannah took over the

---

2. The name appears in Leeds Parish Church records, in 1635.

3. Records of the Court Baron of Headingley, 1806. WYAS Leeds, WYL160/220/5. The dip in the land on one side of Shaw Lane still marks the position of the old quarry.

4. Edward Baines, *General and Commercial Directory of the Town and Borough of Leeds*, 1817.

inn in 1818 after the death of Jane Carrett, Joseph Clark insisted that the name should be changed to 'The Old Original Oak', presumably to avoid any confusion with its competitor opposite, 'The Skyrack', which had also called itself after the oak tree. He may have taken the name from the notice nailed to the tree, which declared it to be 'The Original Oak from which the wapentake is named Skyrack.' The inn was listed as 'The Old Original Oak' in Baines's 1822 Directory – with 'Original' in italics for emphasis – but continued to be known more generally just

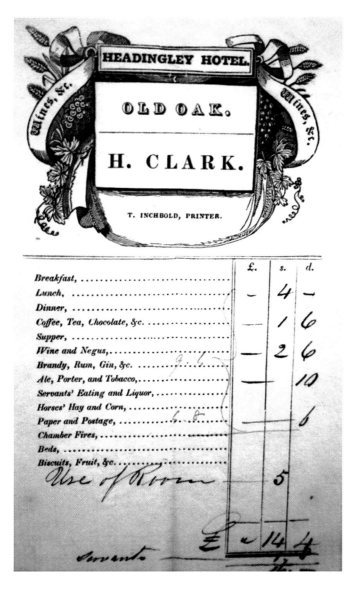

A bill from the Original Oak Inn in 1829, when it styled itself the Headingley Hotel. Hannah Clark was the innkeeper for over forty years. This bill relates to one of the series of meetings held at the inn between 1829 and 1834 in connection with the enclosure of the common land in Headingley. *(West Yorkshire Archive Service, Leeds)*

as 'The Oak Inn' or 'The Old Oak'. More than a century later, around 1940, the old name 'The Original Oak' was revived and since then it has stuck.

Under the management of the Clarks in the 1820s the inn flourished, benefiting no doubt from the growth and increasing prosperity of the village. The front part of the old house was rebuilt to make more space and the inn was restyled 'The Headingley Hotel'. It was too near the town to be a coaching inn, but it offered bedrooms, a full range of food and drink, including ale from its own brewhouse, and stabling for horses. After Joseph Clark's death in 1825,[5] Hannah Clark carried on as licensee and developed the business further, adding more stables and 'a dining-room for Societies'. The many alterations and additions which were made over the years are still reflected today in the patchwork of rooflines and stonework of the pub, and the stables are still there in the yard behind.

The inn became an important focal point for local meetings and events. Almost all the public meetings associated with the Headingley enclosure were held there over the period 1829–34. It was the place for local auction sales, for political meetings, for societies and clubs. The annual dinners which Lord Cardigan as Lord of the Manor provided for his tenants were held there. Indeed, until the new Parochial Institute was opened in Bennett Road in 1884, the inn, together with the Skyrack opposite, provided the only rooms in Headingley village for large meetings. This caused a fierce row in the run-up to the 1841 borough election, when the Liberals accused the Tories of booking all the available rooms in the Original Oak and the Skyrack in advance, leaving the Liberals with nowhere to call a meeting for local residents.[6]

---

5. Aged 58. His wife Hannah lived to be 82 and died in 1861. They are both buried in St Michael's graveyard, with five of their children who died in infancy.

6. *Leeds Mercury*, 31.7.1841. George Hayward the Cardigan agent who lived in Headingley Hall (Tory) and Edwin Eddison, the Town Clerk (Liberal), also a Headingley resident, got into a slanging match over this, and over the location of the polling booth.

In 1847 a further lease was granted by the Cardigan estate to Hannah Clark. As well as the inn, outbuildings, garden and bowling green (mentioned for the first time in this lease), some fourteen acres of grazing land were still included, mainly the same fields along Kirkstall Lane which had been rented long ago in 1711. But change was just round the corner. In 1850 the Cardigan estate, in need of ready money, began to sell off much of the land it owned on the Moor and around the village, and offered some of its tenants the opportunity to buy the property they occupied at a negotiated price.[7] In 1852 the inn was sold to Hannah Clark and her son, but now without the associated land, so finally breaking the link with its old agricultural past. It was sold again in 1865 to a later landlord, James Waddell, and in 1876 was put up for sale by public auction. The sale particulars[8] describe a flourishing business: the inn itself, a brewhouse, stables, coachhouse, clubroom, outbuildings, yards, garden and bowling green. All the fittings – the counters, long seating, bar pumps, brewing pans etc. – were for sale, together with the horses, carriages and cabs: the inn had been running a hackney coach service for the many new residents of Headingley who could not afford their own horse and carriage. The inn was sold for the substantial sum of £8,500. The cab business was later sold on as a separate business but was still run for a time from the inn yard.[9]

The inn had a high reputation. Writing towards the end of the century, local historian William Wheater, who lived in Headingley, recalled the convivial company at the Oak in the 1850s and 60s, when 'everyone who was anyone' would gather there for a drink and conversation.

7. Letter from George Hayward to E.R.Clark, WYAS Leeds, WYL160/220/248.

8. Particulars of Sale, The Oak Inn, auctioned 3.5.1876, WYAS Leeds, WYL160/Deed Packet 1706.

9. See Kelly's Directory of 1888 and 1893. Michael Rayner bought the cab business and continued to run it from the inn until he transferred to St Michael's Lane.

Some of the foremost Leeds merchants were regulars and had their own seats in the bar, the older men dressed in the 'Leeds uniform' of the time: ruffled shirts and suits of best black cloth, worn with the waistcoat open and a swallow-tail coat. The two Members of Parliament who lived locally[10] sometimes called in, as well as merchants from the town who braved the journey along the ill-lit road across Woodhouse Moor and up the rutted turnpike road to Headingley, to enjoy the camaraderie of the Oak.

A menu from 1879 gives an idea of the range of food offered by the dining room, alongside an extensive wine list:

Soups – Clear and Mock Turtle

Removes – Saddle of Mutton; Calf's Head; Roast Chicken; Boiled Leg of Lamb; Tongue; Boiled Chicken; Roast Beef; Ducklings; Pigeon Pie

Sweets – Cabinet Pudding; Lemon Pudding; Custards; Fruit Tarts; Cheesecakes; Blancmange and Jellies; Ice Puddings; Cheese and Salad.

You could dine well at the Oak.

A special feature of the inn was its bowling green and the associated Bowling Club. It was claimed by Club members that the green was very ancient in origin but this seems to have been wishful thinking: there is no supporting evidence. However, it is known that the green existed in 1847, perhaps created from the garden next to the inn. The Club may have come into existence around the same time, though its formal foundation was rather later.[11] It had its own clubroom in the inn with its trophies on display and was highly successful, with over 100 members at its peak and a full calendar of competitive matches. It achieved some fame in 1888 when the team won the Plymouth Cup at the Tercentenary Commemoration of Drake's famous match at Plymouth, a victory they celebrated annually with

---

10. James Garth Marshall, MP, who lived at Headingley House, and George Skirrow Beecroft, MP, of Abbey House, Kirkstall.

11. Around 1868. Records of the Original Oak Bowling Club from 1868 to 1970 are held by the WYAS, Leeds, ref. OO/BC

a match and a dinner afterwards. The pub still has a bar called the 'Plymouth Lounge', an echo of this famous conquest. The Club went on playing at the Oak through-out the next century until 1998 when, amid much public protest, the bowling green was finally dug up to provide outside drinking space for a new and rather different clientele.

After the sale in 1876 the inn had a number of different landlords who lived on the premises together with the serving staff, but from 1903 it enjoyed another long period of continuity: it was bought by James Laycock whose family continued to own and run it for over 50 years. It was finally taken over by Tetley's in the 1950s and is now owned by M& B of Birmingham. Long popular with the cricketing fraternity and now packed with crowds of students and young people, it is said to be one of the five most successful pubs in the country.

The Oak Bowling Club team from Headingley in Elizabethan costume, photographed in 1888 at Plymouth when they won the Plymouth Cup at the Tercentenary Commemoration of Drake's famous match on Plymouth Hoe. *(Thoresby Society)*

A view of the Original Oak Inn around 1890. The two-storey extension to the right of the main building at this time still has a ground floor, later removed and replaced with supporting pillars in order to provide better access to the stable yard at the back. The inn still has its sign over the central door, later blanked out. *(Godfrey Bingley collection: reproduced with the permission of Leeds University Library).*

THE SKYRACK

The origins of the Skyrack were rather different from the
Original Oak. It too was owned by the Cardigan estate,
but in the nineteenth century Cardigan rent accounts it
was always included in the list of 'cottages', the small
houses built by villagers on scraps of waste land, and the
annual rent was correspondingly small: only 6s. a year even
in the late 1850s, just before it was sold. There were many
of these cottage encroachments during the late eighteenth
century, particularly on what was left of the village green,
near to the church (St Michael's) in the heart of the village.
These unauthorised cottages were permitted in return for
a few shillings rent paid annually to Lord Cardigan, in
recognition of his rights as Lord of the Manor, but there
was no lease or security of tenure. The Skyrack inn must
have originated in such a cottage, built by some
enterprising villager on a small plot of waste ground on the
verge of the turnpike road.

There is no clear record of when it was built, though it
looks from John Tuke's map of 1781 that it may already
have been in existence by then. It seems to have been built
originally as one large double-fronted house – surprisingly
grand for a cottage – but at some very early stage an
extension, slightly lower and shallower, was added to the
side to create a separate residence, perhaps in order to allow
room for part of the main house to be used as an inn.
It stood in an ideal position for passing and local trade:
right next to the main turnpike road to Otley, at the
junction with the routes from Headingley down to
Kirkstall and Burley, and set at a prominent angle visible
from all directions. It was and still is a handsome stone
building, and from the front it has remained remarkably
unchanged over some 200 years,[12] since its picture was
painted in the early years of the nineteenth century (p.125).

12. In 1878 there was a proposal to add bay windows to the front of
the building, but this was never carried out (WYAS Leeds, Building
Plans 1878/38).

This painting suggests that only part of the main building was then used as an inn; the other part was marked off by a low front wall and had a small railed forecourt or garden and a separate front door. The inn itself may have been fairly small at first, just one or two rooms.

It seems clear that the inn was already in business by around 1810, and in 1817 it was listed in Baines's Directory of Leeds as the Skyrack (also spelt Skirake) Inn. Like the Original Oak, it was named after the ancient Shire Oak tree just across the road, Headingley's main claim to fame. It has retained that name ever since, though the tree itself has perished and the significance of the name has been mainly forgotten.

Perhaps reflecting its more humble origins, the Skyrack did not enjoy the prestige of the Original Oak opposite, at least in its early years, nor could it offer the same facilities. No doubt it served a rather different clientele, the village working men and labourers rather than the merchants and landowners. It did not aspire to be a hotel like its competitor, though by 1840 it had expanded enough to offer a room for meetings. In the early years of the century it had a succession of different landlords and may have had a rather dubious reputation. In 1850 the landlord of the time, John Parker, got into considerable trouble for allowing gambling on the premises every night. He was summoned before the Magistrates, and Lord Cardigan's agent, George Hayward, sent him a stiff letter, accusing him of failing to 'conduct the house in a respectable manner', and warning him that he would be given notice to quit if there was no improvement.[13] He must have toed the line after this, for he continued as landlord for some years and in 1862 was able to take over the inn from the Cardigan estate.

We can get an idea of what the inn was like in 1888 from the description given when the Cardigan estate finally sold off its remaining interest. By now it was a

---

13. WYAS Leeds, WYL160/220/26, letter from George Hayward to James Parker, 7.2.1850.

substantial establishment, occupying the whole house. The bar, smoke room, commercial room, sitting room, tap room and kitchen occupied the ground floor; upstairs there was accommodation for the licensee and family, with three bedrooms and a lodging room for any overnight visitors; in the yard behind stood various outbuildings, including a warehouse, two-stall stable, brewhouse, and coachhouse. The jumble of rooflines is still visible behind the pub today. One of the outbuildings, now incorporated into the main building, housed a small shop with a narrow frontage to the main road and a bow window, let to a boot and shoe-maker. The adjoining cottage and garden (now all part of

The Skyrack, around 1810. It was already an inn: the painted sign can be seen over the door. The extension on the left was a separate residence with its own door and small enclosed garden. *(Thoresby Society)*

The Skyrack in a postcard of around 1905, remarkably unchanged over the previous century.

the pub) was apparently still rented out separately. Living over the pub must have been rather a tight fit for Mary Buckle, the licensee at the time, for she had eight children and her brother living with her at the inn as well as the occasional lodger.

The inn became the home for a number of local societies. Kelly's Directory of Leeds for 1888 lists the Headingley Branch of the Stonemasons' Society (a friendly society specifically for stonemasons – an indication of how many there were in the village, working in the nearby quarries); a branch of the Oddfellows; the Headingley Football Club; and the Headingley United Cricket Club. The village still had a strong sense of community, with many flourishing groups of local working men, and the pub provided them with a convivial meeting place.

Over the following century, the pub was extended and developed, absorbing the various outbuildings and making full use of its restricted site to provide space for the pressing needs of its new youthful clientele. Its cottage origins seem very distant now.

THE TOWN SCHOOL

TEACHING THE CHILDREN

THE PARISH CENTRE in St Michael's Road, just across from the church, was once the Headingley 'Town School', later known as St Michael's Primary School, its origins clear from its tall-windowed architecture and the stone door lintel in St Michael's Lane still headed 'Boys' School'. The main part of the building dates from 1844, with extensive later additions. The origins of the school, however, lie earlier, in the late eighteenth century.

In 1764, when the curate of Headingley reported on his chapelry to his Archbishop,[1] he noted that there was no charity or public school there, just a 'petty' school to instruct the small children in the Christian religion. Some years later, in 1783, action was taken to remedy this. Subscriptions were collected from local people for the building of a schoolroom and master's house, to provide schooling for poor children in the township. The Lord of the Manor, the Duke of Montague (the senior title of the Earl of Cardigan at the time) had to be approached for permission to build on a piece of the common land in the middle of the village, part of the village green, and for a

1. *Archbishop Drummond's Visitation Returns 1764*, Return for Headingley (Borthwick Institute of Historical Research, Texts and Calendars 23, Vol.II).

The Disbursements of Joseph Kirk for
Building a House and Schoolhouse at Headingley

	£	s	d
Paid Mr Waddington for Lading Lime & Stone	2	14	0
Do George Smith	3	14	6
Do Joseph Kirk for Leading Stone Slate Brick			
Timber Flaggs ... Earth and Sand	5	19	0
To paying Helen for Removing Clay	–	1	–
To Setting out ye Ground work	–	2	6
To 8 Days work to Joseph Corret	–	10	8
To Hartley for digging ground work & laying ye brick	–	10	6
To paying floor pot	–	2	6
Paid the Schoolmaster for surveying & measuring the works	–	10	6
Do James Procter for Land to C gave the Settlement	–	2	6
Do for Meal and Drink at the Raising	–	9	–
Do to Hartley and Son 1 Day filling Earth	–	2	6
Do for Nails brags and Latts	1	1	2
Do for a Watering pan	–	3	6
Do Slating pott & Do for Lead	–	3	9
Do to Robison for Lime	1	1	–
Do to th of Paint	–	7	–
Do to Oil and Bladder	–	4	1
Do for Wheeling Earth and Carrying out Stones and Levelling the floors for flagging	–	5	–
Do for a Writing Desk Table and other fixtures for the School	1	13	–
Do to James Gray for Glazing	3	3	10
Do for painting	–	10	6
Do to Busfing for 1500 Bricks	–	18	–
Cd ford			

The building account for the school in 1784. The costs for this simple brick and stone building, with its flagged floor, one writing desk and table, a range for warmth, and a 'necessary house' outside, amounted to £100. 6s. 1d. *(West Yorkshire Archive Service, Leeds)*

contribution towards the cost (a Mr Skelton was paid 5s. for writing this important letter). The Duke gave his consent and contributed £50, Benjamin Wade of New Grange gave ten guineas, and a further 26 people gave sums ranging from five guineas down to 2s. 6d. The curate made a late contribution of only half a guinea – this was clearly not a church initiative. A total of £96 12s. 6d. was collected. A schoolmaster had already been found (was he the mover behind the project?), and he helped to supervise the building work, which did not take long to finish. The bill for the work amounted to just over £100, some £4 more than the sum collected.[2] The main expense was materials, as labour came pretty cheap, just over 1s. a day per man.

This first school building was a modest one, a single schoolroom, built of stone, with a slate roof and flagged floor, equipped with a writing desk, a table and probably benches, and with a 'necessary house' (a privy) outside. Attached to it was a small one-up one-down house for the master, with a little fenced-off garden.

The running of the school depended on annual subscriptions. According to a record of a meeting of the subscribers on 6 March 1786[3] two trustees were to be appointed, each serving for two years, elected by those subscribers who had contributed at least two guineas towards the cost of building (so excluding the curate) and were willing to pay 5s. or more annually. For each 10s. subscribed annually the Master was to 'teach one Poor Child one Year to Read (and Write if required)': writing was not viewed as a necessary skill for the poor. In 1786 the twelve subscribers listed were paying a total of £4 2s. annually, so the Master was presumably expected to take on eight poor children, along with any others who could afford a penny or two in fees. His salary depended wholly on subscriptions and whatever parents could afford.

---

2. List of Subscribers and Building Account, WYAS Leeds, RDP39/117.

3. WYAS Leeds, Butler MS/30.

In 1785 a new schoolmaster was appointed, Joseph Brooke, who was to remain in post for some 30 years, followed by his son Benjamin, both of them important figures in the local village community, serving at various times as parish clerk, village constable, surveyor of the highways, and overseer of the poor. In 1797 Joseph Brooke, together with the 'poor inhabitants of the township', petitioned Lord Cardigan and other principal residents for money to enlarge the master's house by adding a room over the schoolroom to make it more comfortable for a family[4] (his wife was expecting a baby at the time). The petition included a proposal which would help to supplement the funding for the school: Thomas Martin, a papermaker based at Wood's Mill on Meanwood Beck, wanted to rent an acre of common land on Headingley Moor to build a reservoir for his mill, the annual rent of five guineas to be paid to the schoolmaster 'for the Education of Poor children, inhabitants of the township.' Lord Cardigan agreed to both proposals and subscribed twenty guineas; others followed suit. The house was enlarged at a cost of £65 12s. 1d., and a lease was duly granted to Thomas Martin, the land having first been vested in eight trustees. The rent was to be applied to the education in reading, writing and arithmetic of six poor children, who were to be elected annually at a vestry meeting held on Michaelmas Day. It is clear that the intention was to make the selection of the children for free schooling as open and democratic as possible.

In 1806 there was a further small supplement to the school's income when Lord Cardigan, with the consent of the other freeholders, gave permission to Thomas Bischoff, the owner of Headingley House, to enclose some waste land 'on the low green' (the corner of the village green between St Michael's Road and North Lane) if he paid a sum of ten guineas to the trustees of the school and one guinea a year thereafter. However, this arrangement lapsed over time and became the subject of a legal dispute in 1835.

---

4. WYAS Leeds, RDP39/118.

It was then discovered that this land and the site of the school itself, also common land, had never been legally granted and conveyed by Lord Cardigan, as Lord of the Manor. So in 1836 action was taken to rectify this: the site of the school and the master's house was conveyed to fourteen trustees, including the Vicar of Leeds and the curate, 'in trust... for the education teaching and instruction of the children of the Inhabitants of the Township in reading writing and accounts' (higher aims than in 1786).[5] The accompanying plan shows the single-roomed school with the small master's house attached, outbuildings to the side, a garden behind, and a triangle of land in front still belonging to Lord Cardigan.

Rebuilding

This small school, known as the Town School, was by the early 1840s inadequate for the needs of the area with its growing population, and the building was old-fashioned and dilapidated: there was a need to rebuild and expand. However, the school faced financial problems. The only regular income was £7 a year; otherwise it relied on subscriptions from local residents and small fees from the children, sometimes subsidised by charitable individuals. There were also problems over the management of the school, in particular the selection of children for free places. Some people felt the new curate, William Williamson, and his 'womenfolk' were far too interfering in school affairs. No doubt dissent was fed by the tension between the growing community of non-conformists and the church – education was a key area. By 1843 feelings were running high and the chairman of the trustees, John Hope Shaw, had to step in.[6] It was at his suggestion that in 1844 the

---

5. WYAS Leeds, RDP39/123.

6. WYAS Leeds, RDP39/127. John Hope Shaw was a distinguished Leeds solicitor, three times Mayor of Leeds: he lived at Shaw House in Shaw Lane, which was named after him (previously the whole road had been called Monk Bridge Road). See R.V. Taylor, *Worthies of Leeds*, Leeds, 1865.

The boys' entrance to the School: the blocked up doorway on St Michael's Lane still has this heading, dating from 1893 when the school reverted to being mixed but with segregated entrances and playgrounds.

school was brought into union with the National Society (for the Education of the Poor according to the Principles of the Church of England), partly with a view to getting a grant towards the cost of rebuilding and partly to avoid further disputes. Effectively the school, founded by the generosity of local residents, was now brought under the wing of the church. Its name was changed to the Town National School and rebuilding was undertaken with a grant from the Society. The old building was demolished, though some of its materials may well have been used in the new school. A large well-lit schoolroom was built, still there today as part of the present building, with a new house for the master to the side and a garden behind. One old man speaking much later in the century remembered the orchard there, where the boys were sent sometimes to pick apples, plums and gooseberries. When he was caught helping himself after school hours that was the end of his schooling!

The education offered was not free for most of the children, though fees were kept as low as possible. In the late 1840s the trustees decided that the school fees should be 3d. a week for the first child and 2d. a week for others, but that 'the children of parents above the labouring and mechanic class should pay 6d. a week, the secretary and treasurer to decide the question of class', an unenviable task. This new idea suggests that the influx of more affluent middle-class families into Headingley was changing the profile of the school. But the differential was soon dropped and the fee, the 'children's pence', continued to be 2d. a week until 1904 when the newly established local education authority ruled that fees should no longer be charged.

In the 1850s there was some concern about numbers as average attendance had fallen to only 40–50 children. While the village population was growing fast, education was not compulsory and many poorer children attended only briefly or sporadically, or just went to Sunday School for basic instruction in reading. Both St Michael's Church and the expanding Wesleyan chapel ran active and well-attended Sunday Schools. There were also two other schools for young children not far away: the Glebe School which the curate and his wife had established in 1840 near the parsonage in Otley Road, built by public subscription with a grant from the National Society (demolished in the 1880s when Burton Crescent was created); and a school for infants at the top of Hollin Lane, also built around 1840 to serve the Far Headingley community.[7] In the same period new church schools were established at Burley, Meanwood, and Kirkstall.

There were also a number of small private 'dame' schools for young children, run by women in their own homes. Frank Meadow Sutcliffe, the Whitby photographer, who was brought up in Headingley, recalled starting out

---

7. The building still exists, now known as Glebe Cottage. The school was transferred to the newly-established St Chad's parish in 1869, and, housed in new buildings, was renamed St Chad's Primary School. It closed in the 1980s. The premises are now used as a private nursery.

A photograph of one of the Town School classes in 1897, outside the school. The tophatted bearded figure at the back is Canon Frederick Wood, vicar of St Michael's 1881–1913. *(West Yorkshire Archive Service, Leeds)*

in the 1860s in a little school in Far Headingley run by a Miss Riley, who combined teaching with attending to her household cooking, the air full of penetrating smells. He felt he did not learn much![8] For the better-off residents there was the option of one of the small private 'academies' of which there were several in Headingley. They could claim a more select clientele and a high level of personal care. One 'seminary for young gentlemen under the age of eight' in Headingley offered the 'gentle Discipline of the Instructress together with the Attentions of the Mother', for a sum of £4 10s. a quarter,[9] attractive to devoted parents but expensive. In addition to schools for younger children, there were several private schools taking boarders, including young ladies who might be taught not only reading, grammar and arithmetic but such 'elegant and fashionable arts' as painting on satin and velvet.[10] The National School contented itself with plenty of useful needlework for the girls.

Education for All – The Board School

From 1857, under a new headmaster, the National School prospered and numbers built up, but major changes were on the horizon. Following the 1870 Education Act, elementary education was made compulsory in 1880 for all children from age 5 to 13 (10 for those who had already achieved the basic standard and needed to work). Children who had never attended school before arrived at the door. At first the school coped with the increasing numbers, but it soon became clear that it could not provide for all the children in this expanding suburb, even allowing for those who were taught privately or sent away to school (there were quite a number in this well-heeled area). So in 1881

---

8. Michael Hiley, *Frank Sutcliffe, Photographer of Whitby*, Phillimore, 2005.

9. Advertisement in the *Leeds Mercury*, 7.1.1837.

10. Advertisement for Mrs Maria Snell's Ladies' Seminary, Headingley, *Leeds Mercury*, 9.6.1827.

the newly-established Leeds School Board[11] decided to build a new elementary school for Headingley, on a vacant site in Bennett Road which was then being opened up. The Board, believing in the need to segregate the sexes, put forward a proposal for a scheme of reorganisation whereby the National School would take only boys and the new Board School would take girls and infants, and after some debate the National School trustees agreed. One suspects that they might not have been so amenable if they had been asked to have the girls instead of the boys.

The Board School opened its doors in 1882 in a large and commodious building designed by the School Board

The Board School (later Headingley County Primary School) in Bennett Road, which opened in 1882 in this handsome building, which had to be extended to the side in 1905 to accommodate growing numbers. It was vacated in 2006 when the school merged with St Michael's School. The hope now (2008) is to raise funds to convert it for community use (the HEART project).

---

11. For more information on the work of the School Board, see the Board's Triennial Reports from 1870 onwards (copies in Leeds Local Studies Library). The Board faced the task of providing school places for more than half the 59,000 children aged between 3 and 13 in the borough. Headingley was not initially a priority area.

architect, Richard Adams, to the latest educational standards, with a spacious hall and classrooms, glazed partitions, large windows, cloakrooms and lavatories. Built of stone, plain and severe in design (cost was a factor), it was and is a rather grand and imposing building, symbolic of the Board's pride in its achievements.[12] The girls and infants who had attended the National School transferred to the new school amid a certain amount of grumbling, and new children who had never been to school before began to arrive at both schools. They were rigorously inspected for cleanliness and some sent outside to the tap.

Over the next few years it is clear that a measure of rivalry flourished between the two schools, with the National School claiming the higher ground in terms of academic standards and religious ethos, while the Board School could claim better premises and facilities, a modern approach, and rigorous standards of inspection. The need for better premises was indeed a serious issue for the National School and in 1888 its building was extended to the rear to provide two additional classrooms. Five years later, in 1893, the Leeds School Board changed its policy on segregation in favour of mixed classes, as it was thought that the girls had a 'refining influence' on the boys, and it was agreed that both schools should become mixed. There was room enough, at least initially, at Bennett Road, but at the National School further alterations were urgently needed to accommodate girls and infants in addition to the boys. The schoolmaster's house was demolished and replaced with a new building to house the 'babies' and infants; the garden was paved over to create a new playground for the girls, safely segregated from the boys; and separate entrances for boys and girls were provided. A bell-cote for the school bell was set on the roof of the extension and the building assumed the appearance it has today. By 1900 the school was able to accommodate about 370 children.

12. In 1905 a substantial addition was built to the side to provide more space, unbalancing the building's symmetry.

For many Headingley children, before the introduction of compulsory secondary education after the Second World War, this school, like the Bennett Road School, provided all the education they received.

In 1925, when numbers appeared to be falling, the local authority suggested a merger of the National School and the Board School, with the infants and younger children housed in the National School and the older children in the larger, more modern premises in Bennett Road. The trustees of the National School declined and both schools were allowed to continue and retain their separate identity. Names changed over the years: the National School became St Michael's Church of England Primary School (Voluntary Aided) and the Board School became Headingley County Primary School. In 1978 St Michael's School transferred to new purpose-built premises on a site in Wood Lane, behind the Arndale Centre. After a public appeal for funds, the old school building was adapted to a new life as the Parish Centre.

Postcard view of St Michael's School in the 1950s. The School moved to new premises in Wood Lane in the 1970s and funds were raised to convert the old building for use as a Parish Centre. *(Thoresby Society)*

Over recent years, as Headingley has changed from family occupation into a place dominated by students, school rolls have inevitably dropped and the proposal to merge schools has been resurrected, this time involving the closure of the Bennett Road site and the transfer of the children to St Michael's. This took place in the Autumn of 2006. A new name has been chosen to symbolise the coming together of the two schools, providing a link with Headingley's history: Shire Oak Church of England Primary School (now Voluntary Controlled). As for the Bennett Road premises, it is hoped that they can be retained and used to serve the local community, and a comprehensive plan has been put forward which at the time of writing is still under consideration.

A Patch of Green

One feature outside the Parish Centre has a special resonance and deserves a second look. The charming, well-tended garden to the front, a small oasis in the asphalt environment, is all that remains now of the former village green. When the site of the old Town School was conveyed to the school trustees by Lord Cardigan back in 1836, this small piece of the common land was retained and was only transferred to the trustees 50 years later in 1888, when Lady Cardigan agreed to sell it for the nominal sum of eight guineas, at the time when almost all the Cardigan property left in Headingley was coming up for sale. Even then, as late as 1888, its origins were remembered: a plan of the school of the same date shows the land as 'Town Green'.[13] Today only this small garden remains as a reminder of the former green space on which the original charity school was built.

The garden in front of the former school, all that remains now of the original Headingley village green.

13. WYAS Leeds, RDP39/138B.

THE GATE HOUSE

THE MARSHALLS, HEADINGLEY HOUSE AND HEADINGLEY LODGE

JUST OFF NORTH Lane, along South Parade, stands a small stone gatehouse with gingerbread decorations, a stone-slab roof and tall chimneys, out of place among the surrounding red brick. This little house is all that remains of the substantial Headingley House estate which during the nineteenth century extended along the northwest side of North Lane and Kirkstall Lane, from what is now the Lounge Cinema site down to the junction with Queenswood Drive, occupying the wooded slopes up to the neighbouring New Grange estate, now Beckett Park. For much of this time it was the estate of the wealthy and influential Marshall family who ran the massive flax-spinning business of Marshall & Co. in Holbeck, and who played a significant part in local Headingley affairs as well as in the wider world. Their great Egyptian-style mills, Temple Mills, built 1838–43, still stand in Marshall Street, Holbeck, an enduring memorial to their immense success, prosperity and confidence.

HEADINGLEY HOUSE

The origins of the Headingley House estate are earlier. In 1803 part of this land, some thirteen acres, was bought by

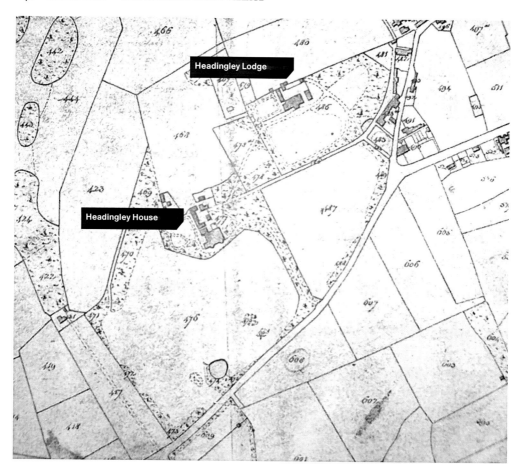

Extract from the 1846 Tithe Map showing the position of Headingley House and Headingley Lodge. The field boundary behind the Lodge was to become Ash Road when the adjoining land was sold for building in 1888. The drive up to the House from Kirkstall Lane became the line of Headingley Avenue when the grounds of the House were sold for development in 1900. *(National Archives, Kew)*

Thomas Bischoff, a merchant banker from the town, together with his brother James Bischoff, a wool merchant.[1] They bought the land from another of the Leeds gentlemen merchants, John Lee.[2] Thomas Bischoff

---

1. They were members of a well-known family of merchants in Leeds. Their grandfather Bernard Bischoff, from Basle, had settled in Leeds in the early eighteenth century, been naturalised, and established a successful business dealing in cloth. Thomas's brother James lived in London where he was an influential figure in the wool trade; he may have helped financially with this purchase.

2. John Lee seems to have acted as an intermediary. He bought one part of the land in 1802/3 from two local men, a clothier and a maltster, and the other part from Christopher Bramley of Woodhouse Lane. The title to the land dates back to 1689, when Thomas Atkinson sold nine closes of land to John Browne of Guisburn (Marshall Deeds, WYAS Leeds, WYL160/68).

was said in the purchase deed to be already renting the land and perhaps had by then begun building a grand house for himself. He was one of the first merchants to make the move from the worsening conditions of life in the town to the pleasant villages around, out in the country but near enough for daily travel into town. A typhus epidemic in 1802 in the middle of town, affecting the wealthy as well as the poor, may have given him an impetus. The house he built was called Headingley House, for a hundred years one of the finest residences in the village but now unknown except for some illustrations. It was demolished at the start of the twentieth century.

Thomas Bischoff was owner of the 'New Bank' which had opened in Boar Lane in 1777. It was destined to collapse 50 years later, in 1827, but at the turn of the century he must have felt confident enough to undertake the building of a handsome country mansion for himself and his family. The house was clearly meant to be a residence of some grandeur, with stables and outbuildings, set in its own park, but still with fields around producing vegetables – he could assume the role of gentleman farmer. The house was home to Thomas and his family for the first few years, but it looks as though he was fairly soon besieged by money problems (his bank was not prospering). In 1811 he mortgaged the house and land, along with some other property, and rented the house out to Alderman Thomas Ikin, another cloth merchant from the town, while he himself went to live in the family house in Woodhouse Lane.

Seven years later, in 1818, presumably in need of capital, he sold the house and all the surrounding land for £7,500 to his neighbour and family friend John Marshall,[3] the immensely successful and wealthy flax-spinner, who at

John Marshall 1765–1845. From a modest start in his father's draper's business in Mill Hill he built a massive flax-spinning empire using the new technology pioneered by Matthew Murray, with whom he was briefly in partnership. He moved to Headingley in 1805, the year when he sat for this portrait. He was already immensely wealthy and successful, but is portrayed here not as the tough, powerful businessman but as the thoughtful man interested in learning. *(Reproduced by permission of the University of Leeds)*

---

3. Marshall Deeds, op. cit.: Indentures of 18.12.1811 (mortgage) and 9.5.1818 (sale). Thomas Bischoff did not return to Headingley, but members of the family bought further land there in the 1820s. After the collapse of his bank in 1827 his fortunes revived: he became the Leeds agent of the Bank of England, with a fine house and business premises in Boar Lane.

that time was renting New Grange. They knew each other well, shared a number of interests, and were both Unitarians linked with Mill Hill Chapel. (This did not preclude attendance at Headingley chapel: Thomas Bischoff's named pew was included in the sale.)

John Marshall[4] had moved to Headingley from Meadow Lane in 1805 and taken on the tenancy of New Grange from the trustees of the Wade estate. New Grange was the finest mansion in the neighbourhood. 'Without pretending to compete with the mighty Harewood in its outside form' claimed the prospectus when it came up for sale later, in 1829, 'it will not yield to it in its internal comfort and arrangement... it soars far above any one in its immediate vicinity'.[5] It was set in an extensive park (the whole estate comprised some 450 acres), with wonderful views over the valley of the Aire, still beautiful then, and the romantic ruins of Kirkstall Abbey. The old mansion is now part of the premises of Leeds Metropolitan University in Beckett Park. It retains its stone balcony to the front, described in 1829 as 'perhaps especially intended for the members of the County to address the admiring Auditory after a successful Poll'. It did indeed house more than one Member of Parliament, though whether they ever addressed admiring listeners from the balcony is open to question.

John Marshall was 40 by the time he moved to Headingley in 1805 and he had a growing family: he and his wife Jane already had seven children and more were to follow. He had married Jane Pollard, a distant cousin, daughter of a Halifax merchant, in 1795. It was perhaps Jane who first introduced him to the Lake District, where they chose to spend their honeymoon. It was a landscape that he grew to love more then any other. Jane knew

Jane Marshall (nee Pollard), 1770–1847, daughter of a Halifax merchant and a lifelong friend of Dorothy Wordsworth. When she and John Marshall married in 1795 they spent their honeymoon in the Lake District, and later, on advice from the Wordsworths, bought a substantial property on Ullswater, which became their principal, much-loved home. *(Reproduced by permission of the University of Leeds)*

4. For full information on John Marshall and his business, life and family see: W.G.Rimmer, *Marshall's of Leeds, Flaxspinners 1788–1886*, Cambridge University Press, 1960.

5. Particulars of Sale of the New Grange Estate, auctioned in London on 29 October 1829 (Thoresby Society).

the Lake District well, as she had been a friend since childhood of Dorothy Wordsworth, William Wordsworth's sister. Dorothy had been sent to Halifax when she was seven, after the death of her mother, to live with an aunt, and the two girls, of similar age, had become friends and remained lifelong correspondents. Jane and John Marshall visited the Wordsworths and became part of their circle of friends. When the Marshalls moved to Headingley, Dorothy wrote to Jane to say how pleased she was that they were moving away from the town, where disease and terrible epidemics posed an ever-present threat to the children of the family: 'I am happy to think that you are got into a country residence…'[6]

Moving to Headingley, then, represented a change to a healthier environment for the family, but it also meant a shift upwards in social status, and at New Grange John Marshall threw himself with enthusiasm into the pursuits of a country gentleman. He took an interest in the farm on the estate, reared sheep, selected and designed plantations of trees in his grounds, representing, so it is said, the battle lines at Waterloo. (Tree planting became an enduring hobby of his. William Wordsworth was later to seek his advice on planting in his own garden.) His household continued to increase, five more children being born after the move to New Grange, making twelve in all. Some of Jane's family also came to live with them and a large retinue of servants was needed to support the establishment. The rent was high, and the costs of the household very considerable, but he was a very wealthy man. It seems to have been a happy family home. In 1807 the Wordsworths came to visit them, and Dorothy described their weekend: '… we stayed from Friday till Monday morning. It is a cheerful, pleasant place, and the

---

6. Letter of 2 June 1806 from Dorothy Wordsworth to Jane Marshall: E.de Selincourt (ed), *The Collected Letters of William and Dorothy Wordsworth*, Oxford, 1937. Dorothy was very conscious of the risks to which children were exposed, having nursed a baby niece who died.

Abbey – how beautiful!'[7] They clearly enjoyed their visit and Dorothy wrote that they often spoke of it afterwards with pleasure.

A Move

However, John Marshall's ambitions were already ranging further afield. He decided to look for an estate to purchase in their beloved Lake District, one that would give him the social status he sought. He enlisted the help of the Wordsworths, Coleridge and other Lakeland friends in trying to find 'a beautiful estate of 200 acres' in the Lakes. By 1815 he had bought a house and land at Ullswater called Hallsteads, and this in due course became the main family home.[8] It was still necessary, however, to maintain a home in Leeds in order to continue to manage the immense business which was the source of the family wealth. He decided that continuing to rent New Grange was too expensive, but the family wanted to remain in Headingley. So in 1818 John Marshall bought the neighbouring Headingley House from his friend Thomas Bischoff. The estate was smaller and more manageable than New Grange but the house was handsome enough and set in pleasant parkland where he could pursue his interest in landscape design. It was to remain in the Marshall family for the next 70 years.

John Marshall extended the house in 1819 at considerable expense, adding a new wing to provide additional accommodation for his large household. Although the family spent much of their time in the Lake District, particularly in the summer, and they also had a house in London, their Headingley home was maintained

---

7. Letter of 19 July 1807 from Dorothy Wordsworth to Catherine Clarkson, *Collected Letters*, op.cit.

8. John Marshall was later to buy or assist with the purchase of property for each of his sons in the Lake District, with the result that the family owned vast swathes of land there. Much of it is now owned by the National Trust.

in style, costing over £3,000 a year to run.[9] One gets a sense of its size from the description provided in 1888, when it was put up for sale: eight reception rooms, including a library, a schoolroom, and a billiard and smoking room, and twelve principal bedrooms, dressing rooms, a nursery, and six servants' rooms; a substantial establishment. Over the years additional land was purchased from the neighbouring landowners, Lord Cardigan and William Beckett, so that the estate consisted in all of some 36 acres, mostly 'pleasure grounds, artistically laid out'.[10]

In 1826 John Marshall was elected Member of Parliament for Yorkshire (Leeds itself still had no separate representation). This was at a time when it was almost unprecedented for a manufacturer to be a candidate for election, rather than members of the aristocracy or landed

Headingley House, painted by W.R.Robinson in 1849. The house, built around 1803, was bought by John Marshall in 1818. He added a new west wing, visible on the left of the house, to accommodate his large family and retinue of servants. After further purchases of land, his estate extended along the northern side of North Lane/Kirkstall Lane from the site of the Lounge down to Langdale Terrace. His family continued to own and live in the House until 1888 when it was put up for sale. (*Leeds Library and Information Services*)

9. W.G. Rimmer, op.cit.

10. Particulars of Sale, Headingley House Estate, 30 May 1888 (Thoresby Society).

THE NEW

"House that Jack Built,"

HUMBLY DEDICATED TO

MR. JOHN MARSHALL,

FLAX SPINNER, HOLBECK.

This is the House that Jack Built.

This is the Flax all heckled and torn, that lays in the House that Jack built.

These are the Children all forlorn, who toil and slave from night till morn, in spinning the Flax, all heckled and torn, that lays in the House that Jack built.

This is the Man all *shaven and shorn*, for whom the poor Children all forlorn, toil and slave from night till morn, in spinning the Flax, all heckled and torn, that lays in the House that Jack built.

This is John Bull, a Freeman born, whom the Man with his head all shaven and shorn, thinks to lead by the nose, by talking of Corn, while the poor Children all forlorn, get so little for toiling from night till morn, in spinning his Flax, all heckled and torn, that lays in the House that Jack built.

This is the *Lord* so very high-born, who treated his LONG WOOL friends with scorn, yet has joined with the Man all shaven and shorn, to lead John Bull by the nose, by *talking* of Corn, but if they don't mind they'll be tossed and torn, or be sent with the Children all forlorn, to twist from the Flax, all heckled and torn, a Rope for to hang themselves some morn, in front of

THE HOUSE THAT JACK BUILT.

John Marshall employed many children in his mills. While he aimed to provide good conditions and schooling for them he was opposed to legislation to control their hours and was accused of exploitation – the theme of this flyer, circulated when he stood for Parliament in 1826. *(Thoresby Society)*

gentry. His election demonstrates the respect with which he was regarded and the importance attached to his being able to represent the growing manufacturing interests of the county. While he faced accusations of exploitation of the children working in his mills, he was by the standards of the time an enlightened employer, providing model facilities for his workers and schools for the children. But he was now over 60 and his health was beginning to trouble him. He did not seek re-election in 1830 and he devoted himself more and more to his other cultural and social interests, particularly in education: he was prominent in the establishment of the University of London (open to Dissenters like himself, which other universities were not) and the promotion of a University College in Leeds. He also spent more and more of his time away from Leeds, in London and the Lakes, leaving his four sons who had entered the business to run it for him.

HEADINGLEY LODGE

His sons initially were based in Headingley House, but when his second son, John Marshall Junior, married in 1828 John Marshall decided to buy a neighbouring property for him to live in. The house he bought was Headingley Lodge,[11] set in grounds adjoining his own but nearer the village centre; it backed onto what is now Ash Road (between Headingley Mount[12] and Derwentwater Terrace), with its gardens running down towards North

Headingley House, drawn by Walter Braithwaite in the late nineteenth century not long before its sale and demolition. *(Leeds Library and Information Services)*

---

11. This house was built about 1814 by Thomas Lee, member of a prominent family of Leeds merchants (Marshall Deeds, op. cit.). However he soon found himself in deep financial difficulties (the family was involved in bankruptcy proceedings) and mortgaged the property in 1821 to Richard Battye, a London lawyer. When Thomas Lee died in 1823 he still owed all the money he had borrowed, and the property was repossessed; it was finally offered for sale by Richard Battye's executors in 1829.

12. A section of old stone wall survives at the top of Headingley Mount, almost certainly part of the garden wall of Headingley Lodge.

Lane. It is said that John Junior would have preferred to buy New Grange instead (it was about to come up for sale) but his father rejected this expensive suggestion. In fact Headingley Lodge and the House fitted together well, forming one estate. A joint entrance to the two houses with a gatehouse was constructed in North Lane opposite the end of St Michael's Road (where South Parade is now), and from there the carriage drive forked, one side leading to Headingley House and the other to Headingley Lodge.

John Marshall Junior was an active partner in the business, together with his brothers, and was to follow in his father's parliamentary footsteps. He was elected one of the first two MPs for Leeds in 1832, when the Reform Act finally allowed the borough to be represented in Parliament.[13] He also took on local roles, taking his turn as Headingley Overseer of the Poor and Surveyor of the Highways among other activities. However, he died in 1836 when he was only 39 years old, 'to universal and profound regret'[14], and Headingley Lodge was then rented out to family friends. In 1846 the tenant was Hamer Stansfield, another cloth merchant and fellow Liberal and Unitarian, and from 1853 until the mid 1860s it was rented by Edward Baines Junior, Editor of the *Leeds Mercury*, which John Marshall had helped to establish.

While Headingley House remained the Yorkshire home of John Marshall until his death in 1845, he was increasingly absent and the house was occupied by his third son, James Garth Marshall, with his family, and by his younger son, Arthur, who never married. (His other son involved in the business, Henry Cowper Marshall, lived a little further out, at Weetwood Hall.) James Garth Marshall was M.P. for Leeds from 1847 to 1852 and later a J.P. and Deputy Lieutenant for the county. Like his father, he took a strong interest in social reform and put

---

13. Liberal MP for Leeds 1832–35. The original petition entreating him to stand in the election, signed by numerous Leeds householders, is in the Thoresby Society collection.

14. R.V.Taylor, *Biographia Leodiensis: Worthies of Leeds*, Leeds, 1865

some of his ideas into effect locally. In 1843, at a time of severe distress because of economic depression, he gave four acres of land in Headingley for garden allotments for the benefit of the working classes, on the principle of a 'Labourers' Friendly Society'.[15] He was a prime mover behind the Headingley Mutual Improvement Society, set up in 1849, which met at the Glebe School and provided evening lectures and study facilities for young men seeking to improve themselves.[16] However, like his father and brothers, his life was divided between Headingley, London and the Lakes, where he had another home at Monk Coniston Hall. He died in 1873, leaving Arthur to live alone in the house, though with a full complement of servants: the 1881 Census[17] shows four servants living in the house and his butler and valet, George Ward, living in the gatehouse.

Departure

Finally, in 1886, after years of decline, the great flax-spinning firm which John Marshall had founded collapsed, and the next generation of Marshalls left Headingley and Leeds for good. In 1888 Headingley House and the surrounding land were put up for sale. Headingley Lodge was not included, as it was sold separately to the current tenant, Thomas Richmond Leuty, another linen manufacturer so presumably well known to the Marshalls. The sale particulars for the auction of the House and its grounds on 30 May 1888 made it clear what the fate of the estate was expected to be: 'The best residential sites

---

15. *Leeds Mercury*, 4.3.1843 and 11.3.1843. JGM gave the land and paid for preparation and drainage etc. and people could then rent the allotments at a small charge. It was reported on 18 March 1843 that Benjamin Gott had followed suit and given eight acres (a touch of competitiveness?). The land JGM gave for allotments now lies under the terraces of the Grimthorpes and the Trelawns.

16. *Leeds Mercury*, 2.2.1850. William Beckett and John Hope Shaw were also supporters. (See p.68).

17. 1881 Census: RG11/4538/87/1.

in Headingley... are now almost all built upon, and consequently this Sale affords an opportunity to a Capitalist or Syndicate of acquiring a Building Estate of great capabilities for profitable development'.[18] It was pointed out that the House could be divided into two or demolished: 'the materials would be valuable in the erection of other houses.' The land was divided into three lots, one consisting of the house and its surrounding park, another a plot of five acres of land used as allotments on the northern side of the estate (presumably including the land given in 1843), and the third a small plot on North Lane where the Lounge Cinema was later to be built

18. Particulars of Sale, Headingley House Estate, 30 May 1888, (Thoresby Society).

Joseph Hepworth (1834–1911), a self-made man, a highly successful entrepreneur in the ready-made clothing trade, with large factories and a chain of shops across the country. He bought Headingley House in 1888 and lived there for 11 years until his retirement. When he left, the estate was put on the market again and sold for development. *(Thoresby Society)*

(1916). The associated plan showed how the site could be developed, with a new road 'authorised by the Corporation' cutting into the estate along an old field boundary: this became Ash Road. The larger plot of land was sold to speculative builders, as expected, but, surprisingly, Headingley House itself did not meet its end at this point. Instead of demolition, the house and its surrounding gardens and park were bought by another well-known Leeds entrepreneur, Joseph Hepworth, who was to live there until the turn of the century.[19]

JOSEPH HEPWORTH

The firm of Joseph Hepworth and Son was, with Montague Burton's, one of the great Leeds success stories in the wholesale manufacture of ready-made clothing. Like John Marshall, Joseph Hepworth was a self-made man, but from humbler beginnings. He had started work as a mill boy, aged 10, in Lindley near Huddersfield, in conditions he later described as not fit for a dog, had moved to Leeds to start his own business but had had to struggle to survive. However, he persevered and, with his son Norris, was the first to pioneer the development of a chain of retail shops to market the garments made in his huge workshops in Wellington Street. In 1891, shortly after his move to Headingley, he opened a new factory in Claypit Lane; by this time he had 107 shops, and was employing over 2,000 workers. His success was based on very large sales at low prices, but not at the expense of his workforce –

19. The changes in ownership of the house over almost a hundred years of its existence mirror the changes in the textile trade in Leeds: built by a member of an eighteenth century family of cloth merchants, it had passed to the owner of the greatest flax-spinning firm of the early nineteenth century, a pioneer in new methods of mechanisation, and then on to one of the first businessmen to exploit the new technology and expanding markets of the mass-produced ready-made clothing trade in the later years of the century. Hepworth's employed many of the workers, predominantly female, who had previously worked in the flax trade before its decline, and even occupied for a time part of the great Marshall Mills at Holbeck.

his workshops were viewed as a model of efficient mechanisation and good working conditions.[20]

Joseph Hepworth lived in Headingley House until the end of the century, when he retired from active involvement in the company he had founded and moved first to Torquay for his health, and then back to Harrogate. Nevertheless he was elected Lord Mayor of Leeds in 1906 and, as a lifelong teetotaller, caused some controversy by refusing to allow alcohol to be served at mayoral functions. He declared that the money thus saved would be given 'for the feeding of poor children during the winter', which must have effectively silenced his critics. He died in 1911, and his life provided the obituary-writers with a model 'rags to riches' story: 'From Mill Boy to Lord Mayor: A Business Romance' was the *Leeds Mercury* headline.[21]

A CHANGING SCENE

Even before Joseph Hepworth moved away from Headingley in 1899, the immediate environment was changing. The house and its gardens were already being hemmed in on one side by the redbrick terraces built on the land which had been sold in 1888. In that sale, no restrictive or protective covenants had been imposed of the kind laid down in the development of other estates such as Cardigan Road or Shire Oak Road to ensure a high standard of building. It was as if the Marshalls, in leaving Headingley behind, shook off all responsibility for what was to follow. Inevitably the speculators chose to build high-density housing for maximum profit, and they moved quickly. By 1889/90[22] Ash Road was under construction and the first

20. Katrina Honeyman, *Well Suited: A History of the Leeds Clothing Industry, 1850–1980*, OUP, 2000.

21. *Leeds Mercury*, 18.10.1911.

22. The 1893 O.S.Map, surveyed 1889/90, shows the stage of construction. In the same period, the Granbys, also including back-to-back houses, are shown being built over the open land and gardens in the triangle between St Michael's Road, North Lane, and Otley Road.

rows of red brick back-to-back terraces, the Trelawns, were being built on its northern side, crowded along streets which ended abruptly at the field boundary. By this date, indeed much earlier, back-to-back houses had been condemned as unhealthy and had been banned in many towns, though not in Leeds. Yet here they were being built with the blessing of the authorities in the rather prestigious neighbourhood of Headingley. The local landscape was changing fast as the century drew to its close.

So it was inevitable that when Headingley House and its park came up for sale again in 1900, it would this time fall into the hands of the developers. The whole estate was bought by Charles Stott of Armley and the site quickly cleared for building. The 1908 OS Map shows the house still in existence but encircled by planned new roads and rows of terraces in course of construction: the Estcourts, Canterbury Drive, Headingley Mount, Headingley Avenue, this last following in part the course of the carriage drive which had been created when the House and the Lodge

Joseph Hepworth & Son's Providence Clothing Factory, Clay Pit Lane, built in 1891 to the highest health and safety standards of the time. Over a thousand people were employed here, mostly female, producing clothes for sale in Hepworth's chain of a hundred 'elegant and magnificently appointed' shops across the country. *(Thoresby Society)*

were separated, leading up from Kirkstall Lane to the entrance to Headingley House. Finally Headingley House itself was demolished. During the First World War development of the site was suspended but then resumed. The green 'undulating slopes' of the park with its plantations of fine trees, which had given a rural aspect to the north side of Kirkstall Lane from the bottom of North Lane down to the junction with Queenswood Drive, disappeared under brick and asphalt. Only the name lingered, borrowed as the name of a house at the far corner of Ash Road, built in 1910.

Headingley Lodge survived much longer. The new owner, Thomas Richmond Leuty, who ran a linen business at Castleton Mills in Armley Road, carried out a number of improvements to the old house in 1887, to update the accommodation. He sold off a corner of his gardens around 1900 for building (Derwentwater Terrace) but

A winter view along Cardigan Road towards North Lane, around 1890. Only one side of Cardigan Road has been built on; land on the other side would be sold off for villa development by the Cricket Football and Athletic Company later in the 1890s. At the junction with North Lane the gatehouse to Headingley Lodge can be seen, before it was moved back to its present position at the top of South Parade. *(Godfrey Bingley collection: reproduced with the permission of Leeds University Library)*

otherwise there was only one change to the arrangements at the Lodge. In 1908, after the sale and demolition of Headingley House, the little gatehouse which had stood in North Lane at the entrance to the joint carriage drive was demolished to make room for the South Parade Sunday School and Chapel, [23] and was rebuilt in its present position, guarding the entrance to the private drive which led up to Headingley Lodge. Thomas Leuty had a busy life: as well as running his business, he was active in politics, served on the Council for many years, was elected Mayor of Leeds in 1893, and was Liberal MP for Leeds East from 1895 to 1900. He was known as a passionate nonconformist and teetotaller. However, he was dogged by ill health and died at the Lodge in 1911, aged only 57. His widow stayed on until the late 1930s. When the Leuty family finally left, the land around the Lodge was sold for infill development (Ash Gardens, Ash Crescent, and Derwentwater Grove). The old house itself survived into the 1950s, and the building which replaced it has kept the name 'Headingley Lodge'.

Memories of Headingley House, Headingley Lodge and their various residents have died away. The only remaining clue is the little gatehouse in South Parade, a leftover from the past, and perhaps the evocative Lake District names of Derwentwater and Langdale given to some of the new streets, a link with the Marshalls' other much-loved landscape to which they finally escaped. The close-packed terraces which took their place remain. For many years they were well-kept family homes, most, including the back-to-backs, with a certain dignity. Now many of them house a fleeting population of students and look sadly unloved.

---

23. For more information on South Parade Church see J.J. Scottorn, *A Short History of South Parade Baptist Church 1779–1979*, Leeds, 1979.

'A WELL-BUILT WALL'

THE ZOOLOGICAL AND BOTANICAL GARDENS

ALONG CARDIGAN ROAD, at the junction with Spring
Road, Bainbrigge Road and Chapel Lane, a small area of
land, now run wild with undergrowth and trees,[1] faces a
section of handsome stone wall which once flanked the
entrance to the Leeds Zoological and Botanical Gardens.
Cardigan Road did not exist then and the gardens spread
to either side, down to Burley Park, all enclosed by high
stone walls which still survive as a curving boundary along
one side of Chapel Lane.

THE VISION

The idea of establishing public gardens in Leeds was
launched in 1837, on the model of similar gardens in other
major cities around the country. The objective was to
provide 'recreation for the people' and 'elevated pastimes
for the operative classes, to wean them from the grosser
pursuits' by offering 'an inducement to spend their hours of

1. This mysterious parcel of land was described as 'waste' in 1846,
when the Tithe Map was drawn up. It was the corner of one of the
fields (Oddy Garth) purchased in 1837 but not needed for the
Gardens. Its present ownership seems obscure (it is not Council
property).

leisure in the pure breeze of the country air.'[2] These were lofty aims but the venture had to be commercially viable too, as this was then the only way to fund such public amenities. A committee was formed to oversee the project and a company was set up to finance it. Shares were offered for sale at £10 each. Shareholders could hope for a return on their money through admission charges if the venture was successful, and they would also have free access to the gardens for themselves and their families. Ambitious plans were drawn up and a bold target of £20,000 was set to finance the project.

The scheme had powerful backing but wider public support was needed. On 22 May 1837 a meeting was called in the Leeds Court House to publicise the project and try to enlist investors. The *Leeds Mercury* in an editorial on 20 May drew attention to the meeting, and its purpose of 'deciding whether Leeds is to have one of these delightful places of public resort, which are now to be found not only in London, but also in Liverpool, Manchester, Bristol, Oxford and Sheffield' (a persuasive appeal to competitive civic pride). The potential financial advantage to investors was stressed as well as public benefit: 'it would certainly be a very great advantage to the inhabitants, by offering a powerful attraction to draw them on summer evenings out of the smoke of the town, and by presenting the greatest facilities and inducements to the study of botany and natural history.' A week later the *Mercury* was able to report that public-spirited citizens had subscribed some £8,800. This, however, was far short of the sum which had been hoped for.

Nevertheless the project went ahead; two possible sites were considered, and the choice fell on Headingley where, to the south of the Leeds-Otley turnpike road, several fields, some 25 acres in all, were available to purchase. This was land which originally had been part of the Bainbrigge

2. Douglas Taylor, 'West Riding Amusement Parks and Gardens', *Yorkshire Archaeological Journal*, 58 (1986).

estate,[3] now split up by inheritance and offered for sale. The land had the advantage of being in 'a pleasant and secluded valley', accessible from Burley as well as the turnpike road through Headingley, and most importantly 'its direction from Leeds is such that it will scarcely ever be reached by the smoke'[4] – the smoke from its multiplying factories and mills was rendering life in Leeds almost intolerable. So the land was purchased for £4,600. A map of the site prepared by Thomas Newsam, Surveyor, shows that the land had other advantages too: there were many mature oak trees, which would help to enhance and shade the gardens, and several natural water courses, all of which could be used to provide water features.

In September 1837 the steering committee advertised for designs for the Gardens, offering a prize of £20 for the best. They received seventeen designs, and chose the one submitted by William Billinton, 'Civil Engineer and Architect,' and Edward Davies, 'Botanist and Landscape Gardener'.[5] Their design, 'proposed to be erected when a sufficient sum has been subscribed', was astonishingly grandiose and elaborate: a magnificent entrance pavilion; conservatories and greenhouses; two lakes complete with islands; walks and terraces; fountains; an orangery and a rosary; an arboretum 'to be distributed in groups according to their genera, as arranged by Linnaeus'; and 'invisible and moveable enclosures for zoological specimens'. If this ambitious scheme had been realised, Leeds would have had public gardens to match the finest in the land.

---

3. Owned partly by Hugh John Marshall (from Barbara Bainbrigge) and R.W.D. Thorp (from Mary Bainbrigge Junior).

4. *Leeds Mercury* 11.7.1840.

5. William Billinton (b.1807) was engineer to the Wakefield Waterworks Co. and practised as an architect and civil engineer in Wakefield. His design for the Gardens seems to have been his most ambitious project. See Derek Linstrum, *West Yorkshire Architects and Architecture*, London, 1978.

A competition was held in 1837 for the design of the proposed Leeds Zoological and Botanical Gardens, and this elaborate and ambitious plan was the winner. In the event not enough money was raised to fulfil the dream, but a simpler cost-cutting version was put into effect. *(Leeds Library and Information Services)*

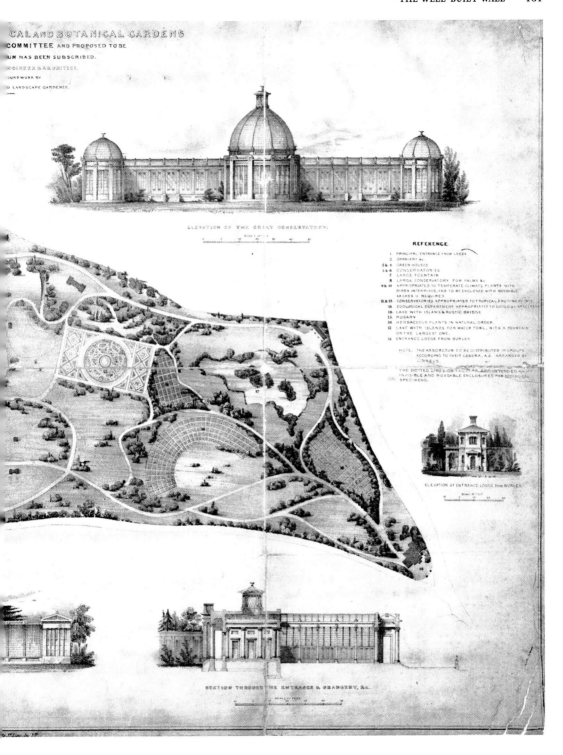

CAL AND BOTANICAL GARDENS
COMMITTEE AND PROPOSED TO BE
UM HAS BEEN SUBSCRIBED.
RCHITECT.
UND WORK BY
LANDSCAPE GARDENER.

ELEVATION OF THE GREAT CONSERVATORY.

REFERENCE.

1.   PRINCIPAL ENTRANCE FROM LEEDS
2.   ORANGERY &c.
3 & 4.   GREEN HOUSES
5 & 6.   CONSERVATORIES
7.   LARGE FOUNTAIN
8.   LARGE CONSERVATORY FOR PALMS &c
9 & 10.   APPROPRIATED TO TEMPERATE CLIMATE PLANTS WITH
         BIRDS INTERMIXED, AND TO BE ENCLOSED WITH MOVEABLE
         SASHES IF REQUIRED.
11 & 12.   CONSERVATORIES APPROPRIATED TO TROPICAL FRUITING PLANTS
13.   ZOOLOGICAL DEPARTMENT APPROPRIATED TO ZOOLOGY SPECIMENS
14.   LAKE WITH ISLAND & RUSTIC BRIDGE
15.   ROSARY
16.   HERBACEOUS PLANTS IN NATURAL ORDER
17.   LAKE WITH ISLANDS FOR WATER FOWL, WITH A FOUNTAIN
      ON THE LARGEST ONE.
18.   ENTRANCE LODGE FROM BURLEY

NOTE. THE ARBORETUM TO BE DISTRIBUTED IN GROUPS
      ACCORDING TO THEIR GENERA, AS ARRANGED BY
      LINNÆUS.

THE DOTTED LINES ON THE PLAN ARE INTENDED AS
INVISIBLE AND MOVEABLE ENCLOSURES FOR ZOOLOGICAL
SPECIMENS.

ELEVATION OF ENTRANCE LODGE FROM BURLEY

SECTION THROUGH THE ENTRANCE & ORANGERY, &c.

The register of shareholders in the Gardens Company[6] shows that the principal supporters of the project were the three wealthy Marshall brothers, sons of John Marshall who had founded the great flax-spinning firm of Marshall & Co. in Holbeck, all partners in the business and resident in or near Headingley, James Garth and Arthur Marshall in Headingley House, and Henry Cowper Marshall at Weetwood Hall. Between them, they held 65 shares. Other well-known Leeds men were involved: William Beckett and Christopher Beckett, the bankers; Edward Baines, the editor of the *Leeds Mercury*, and his son Edward Baines Junior, both friends of the Marshalls; Edwin Eddison, solicitor and Town Clerk, who also acted as clerk to the Gardens committee; Thomas Tatham, another flax spinner, and other merchants of substance. Most of these men were resident in Headingley and within easy reach of the proposed site of the Gardens. However, none of them bought more than twenty shares each, which suggests a certain caution towards the project. The remainder of the shares were bought in small amounts (one, two, five) over a period of time by a wide range of townspeople,

A close-up from the plan for the main entrance. The design for panels in the wall flanking the entrance is echoed in the piece of wall that still stands where Chapel Lane joins Cardigan Road.

6. WYAS Leeds, WYL160/276.

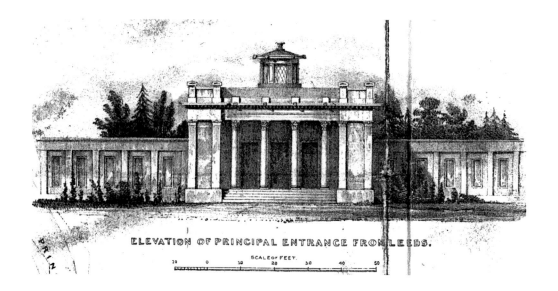

ELEVATION OF PRINCIPAL ENTRANCE FROM LEEDS.

SCALE of FEET.

mostly small businessmen. The list includes woolstaplers, merchants, drapers, a surgeon, an ironmonger, an innkeeper, a coachmaker, a gardener, a stonemason, and so on. In all, £11,140 was raised through the sale of shares, still only a little over half what had been hoped for.

Lack of funds soon put a brake on the zoological ambitions of the committee. George Wombwell, the celebrated London menagerie owner, was approached in 1838 for advice on what animals could be purchased for £1,000 and how much their maintenance would cost. He replied that it depended what was wanted: a pair of lions (which he could provide at the same price as the Manchester Gardens had paid), tigers or panthers were feasible, but elephants would probably be too expensive. A head keeper and two assistants would be needed and there would be the annual cost of feeding and care.[7] All this must have seemed a step too far for the committee, and the rules of the Society were amended to substitute Geology for Zoology in its scientific objectives.

The grand scheme devised by William Billinton also had to be cut back, but enough money remained after buying the land to lay out the gardens with the two lakes and a conservatory, plant the flowerbeds and walks, provide a few specimens of wildlife, and build a high stone enclosing wall with lodges at the Headingley and Burley entrances. (Since there was a charge for admission, the wall had to be high.) A gated access road was created, leading from the main turnpike road from Leeds (Headingley Lane) to the principal entrance: this road still exists as Spring Road.[8] The majority of people were expected to arrive from the turnpike road, either on foot, by carriage or cab, or by the horse-drawn omnibus service initiated in 1838.

---

7. Letter to T.P. Teale from George Wombwell, 12.12.1838. Leeds Local Studies Library, SRQ590.744.L517.

8. So called because of the natural spring there, which had fed a well called 'the Rock', where local people used to be able to go in their carts to draw water. (WYAS Leeds, Oates Family Records, WYL36 – Reminiscences)

LEEDS ZOOLOGICAL AND BOTANICAL GARDENS.

UNEQUALLED ATTRACTION.

The Council have the Pleasure to announce, that on WEDNESDAY, *September First,* 1841, Mr. BYWATER, the unrivalled Pyrotechnic Artist, will exhibit another

DISPLAY OF FIREWORKS,

in the ZOOLOGICAL and BOTANICAL GARDENS, which, for Beauty and Interest, will surpass any previous Exhibition. Amongst other rare Productions will be introduced that *unique* Device the TEMPLE OF PEACE, as exhibited before her Majesty the QUEEN; which, for *Grandeur* and *Effect,* has never yet been surpassed by any Production of the Pyrotechnic Art. As also the grand Napoleonic Piece, introducing the WEEPING WILLOW, as drooping over the Tomb of the departed Emperor at St. Helena, &c. &c. &c.

By the kind Permission of Lieut.-Colonel Marten, the excellent BAND of the FIRST ROYAL DRAGOONS will be in Attendance at *Five o'Clock.*

Firing to commence at Half-past Seven o'Clock, and conclude at Nine.

Admittance, One Shilling each, Children Half-price.

For Particulars see Hand Bills.

A notice in the *Mercury* on 21 August 1841 advertising one of the special spectacles held at the Gardens in the hope of attracting a large attendance. While some events were successful, the Gardens continued to lose money.

THE OPENING

The Gardens were opened to the public on 8 July 1840 with considerable ceremony. A military band played selections of music, and refreshments were provided: confectionery, ices, fruit, wine jellies. The *Leeds Mercury* reported on 11 July: 'The beautiful and retired villages of Headingley and Burley presented a scene of much gaiety and animation on Wednesday last, on the occasion of the public opening of this delightful place of recreation...' It described the Gardens in complimentary terms, but commented that the wildlife was as yet limited to 'a fine pair of swans, some waterfowl, an eagle, a racoon, a fox, some monkeys and tortoises'. About 1,500 people attended the opening, but in true English fashion the morning was marred by a shower of rain. The report concluded rather plaintively that more shareholders were needed to invest in the project, a sign of its continuing financial frailty.

Over the next year efforts were clearly made to enhance the attractions of the Gardens, including the purchase of a bear, but some events were doomed to failure: a planned balloon ascent on 7 October 1840 in front of an expectant crowd of 2,000 people had to be abandoned because the gas supply failed.[9] In May 1841 a new share issue was promoted to try to raise enough money to keep the Gardens going. By 31 July the *Mercury* was able to report that numerous improvements had been made, including a 'habitation for the Bear' and a new summerhouse, and on the previous Wednesday nearly 3,000 people, 'the largest and most respectable company ever known... including many of the principal families of the town', had assembled to walk in the Gardens and enjoy the various attractions: an exhibition of fireworks, a programme of music played by the Band of the 1st Royal Dragoons, and a 'New Zealand Chief', who turned out to be a 'Scotchman' who had visited New Zealand, been inducted as a Chief and bore the

---

9. *Leeds Mercury*, 10.10.1840.

LEEDS ZOOLOGICAL AND BOTANICAL GARDENS.

The Public are respectfully informed that *TO MORROW*, and *EVERY SUCCEEDING SUNDAY*, until further Notice, the GARDENS will be OPEN for ADMISSION BY TICKET ONLY, from Four o'Clock in the Afternoon until Sunset. Tickets, at Sixpence each for Adults, and Threepence each for Children, may be had on Week Days only, of Mr. G. Wood, Confectioner, 145, Briggate, and of Mr. Mearns, at the Gardens. The same Ticket is available for Admission any other Day.

By the kind Permission of Lieut-Col. Marten, K.H., the BAND of the FIRST ROYAL DRAGOONS will attend every WEDNESDAY, from Three to Six o'Clock, until further Notice.

Programme of the Performance on Wednesday next, the 25th Instant :—

PART 1st.

Grand Slow March	by Mohr.
Overture—Pre aux Clercs	Herold.
Valso—Amelia	Schiltz.
No. 1, Air from Pre aux Clercs	Herold.
Du Quel Di—from Anna Bolena	Donizetti.
Pas Redouble—from l'Elisire d'Amore	Donizetti.

PART 2D.

Overture—Semiramide, or Ivanhoe	Rossini.
All's lost—from Sonnambula	Bellini.
Aurora Waltz	Labitski.
Sinfonia Militaire	Piccina.
St. Cloud Quadrilles, dedicated to Prince Albert	Donizetti.
Pas Gallop—from the Grand Ballet of Beniousky,	Bochsa.

&c. &c. &c.

A Grand Display of Fire-Works will take place in the Course of next Month, of which due Notice will be given.

The notice in the *Leeds Mercury* on 21 August 1841 announcing that the Gardens would open on Sunday from now on. This relaxation of Sunday observance aroused much wrath and unleashed a torrent of protest.

tattoos to prove it. But the Gardens were still in financial difficulty, and on the very same day the shareholders in the project announced that the Gardens were losing money and would probably have to be sold at the end of the year.

One problem was the opening hours. A decision had been taken at the planning stage that the Gardens should not be opened on Sundays because that would breach the principles of Sunday observance. However, for many working people this was the only day when they were free to come, and it was reported that this was the reason why it had proved impossible to sell further shares. In August 1841, in an attempt to save the Gardens from closure and sale, a special meeting of the shareholders was called to consider opening the Gardens on Sunday afternoons. In spite of some impassioned arguments against the proposal − in particular that it would lead to drunkenness and dissipation, even though no alcoholic drink was on sale in the Gardens − it was approved by a large majority, though the undoubted financial motive was masked by the argument that Sunday opening would 'advance the moral and religious feeling of the humbler classes' by facilitating their contact with nature. The *Mercury* reported the debate at length[10] and published a long letter from Edward Baines Junior thundering against the decision which had been taken as a 'violation of the Sabbath' and drawing terrifying comparisons with France, Germany and Italy where 'the day is reduced just to the character of a holiday' and music, dancing, cafes, theatres, and worse were all allowed. He envisaged a drunken horde descending on Headingley and a proliferation of public houses to serve them: 'Can it be doubted for a moment that many will return from Headingley on the Sabbath evening staggering…?' (A prophesy fulfilled in modern times?) He was part- icularly outraged by what he saw as the commercial reason for this breach of principle. The following edition saw

10. *Leeds Mercury*, 14.8.1841. Edward Baines resigned from the Council of the Gardens over this issue: letter of 8.9.1841, Leeds Local Studies Library, SRQ590.744.L517.

the publication of opposing arguments, and further correspondence ensued, while various religious groups protested passionately. Nevertheless the Gardens were opened to the public on the Sunday following the shareholders' meeting on the basis agreed, from 4 pm until sunset (2 pm until sunset in winter), but with the proviso that people had to buy their tickets in advance during the previous week – not on some drunken impulse. The new arrangement was publicised in newspaper advertisements.

However, this was not enough to make the Gardens viable. It seems likely that the entrance charge of 6d. for adults and 3d. for children (double for special events such as fireworks) was just too high for the majority of working people, who could have access to open space nearer to the town at Woodhouse Moor, free of charge. Dr Robert Baker, the pioneering medical officer for Leeds, in his 1842 report on conditions in Leeds, which paints a grim picture of the insanitary state of the town and the appalling environment in which the poorer people lived and worked,

TO BE SOLD BY AUCTION,

By Messrs. HARDWICK, on *Monday, the Eighteenth Day of December next*, at Three o'Clock in the Afternoon precisely, at their SALE ROOMS, TRINITY-STREET, LEEDS, subject to such Conditions as shall be then and there produced,

THE LEEDS ZOOLOGICAL AND BOTANICAL GARDENS,

situate in the Township of Headingley-cum-Burley, in the County of York, with the Cottages, Greenhouses, and other Erections thereon, comprising Nineteen Acres.

These Gardens were laid out about Ten Years ago. They are well Drained, and surrounded by a well-built Wall varying from Twelve to Eighteen Feet high. The Trees, Shrubs, and Plants are in thriving Condition, and the whole Establishment, as regards its Water and Aspect, and the Quality of the Soil, will bear comparison with any Gardens in the Kingdom.

The Walks are in good Condition. The Water in the highest part of the Ground is of excellent Quality, and was never known to fail; the Leeds Water Works run immediately adjoining the Upper Part, affording a further Supply of Water if wanted.

The Ponds are in good order, and capable of great extension, if required.

The Property is in every respect suitable for Building Sites, and will be sold at a sacrifice.

For further Particulars apply at the Gardens ; to Mr. Fuller, Nurseryman, Headingley ; to the Auctioneers; or to

PAYNE, EDDISON, & FORD, Solicitors, Leeds.

Leeds, 16th November, 1848.

The notice inserted in newspapers to advertise the forthcoming sale of the Gardens by auction on 18 December 1848. In the event the Gardens were saved and leased to Tommy Clapham the flamboyant showman/entrepreneur in the hope that he could breathe new life into the project. *(Leeds Library and Information Services)*

took this up: 'We have an excellent botanical garden in Leeds failing for want of subscribers, whose use is limited to those who can afford to pay for admission. Is there any reason why this should not also be appropriated once a week gratuitously to the use of the poor and that an annual subscription from the borough rates… should enable the proprietors to afford this gratification to the labouring classes…?'[11] But his proposal was not followed up. The ratepayers of the township were not seeking any additional burdens, and maybe too the proprietors of the Gardens did not really want to share them with 'the labouring classes.'

Closure – 'Under new management'

The Gardens struggled to remain open for a few more years, but finally had to close. Eight years after they had opened, the Company was wound up and the Gardens with all their amenities, including the 'well-built Wall', were offered for sale by auction on 18 December 1848, reported by the *Leeds Mercury* 'with great regret'. They were bought by a banker, James Smith, and then sold on to one of the original movers of the scheme, Henry Cowper Marshall. He leased the Gardens to the entrepreneur showman Thomas Clapham (one of the original shareholders), who reopened them with a new identity as the Leeds Royal Gardens, now open every day, including Sunday, with lower entry charges (2d. normally, 3d. on Gala Days), and with the benefit of a newly opened railway connection direct to the gate at Burley (now Burley Park Station), at a return fare from town of only 3d. (3rd Class). The new line meant that passengers from other places on the line could also visit the Gardens easily, and Tommy Clapham took on the role of railway excursion agent alongside running the Gardens. His advertisement in White's 1853 Directory calls them 'the most beautiful

---

11. R. Baker, *Report on the state and condition of the town of Leeds in the West Riding of the County of York*, Leeds, 1842. Dr Baker had been one of the early supporters of the project.

LEEDS ROYAL GARDENS.

These MAGNIFICENT AND PRINCELY GARDENS are the most beautiful Public Gardens in England. In addition to the Talented Band, there are many other attractions;—they include near 25 Acres of Ground, presenting a rich and varied prospect of graceful hill and dale,—are most beautifully ornamented with Lawns, Walks, Lakes, Trees, Plants, Flowers; aquatic and curious Birds; costly statues; and other curiosities.

Open every Day.

Charges for Admission,—on Gala Days, 3d. or 6d.— other week days and on Sundays, 2d. each. Schools admitted at low rates, by special agreement.

Regular Trains go from the Wellington Station, Leeds, to the Gardens and back, several times every afternoon, which are advertised in the Leeds Northern time bills. Fares to the Gardens and back, 3d. third class, and 6d. first. Passengers can stop at the Gardens every afternoon from Ripon, Harrogate, Arthington, and all other places on the line.

There are also Omnibusses from Leeds to the Gardens and back, every hour.

The Gardens are only one mile and a half from Leeds; persons preferring to walk will enjoy the most beautiful scenery. Tea and other excellent Refreshments can be had in the Gardens for small or large numbers, without previous notice.

Gentlemen and proprietors of public gardens (where gas can be obtained) supplied with a beautiful Balloon and intrepid Æronaut, splendid Fireworks, and other attractions, at reasonable charges.

Address to Mr, Thomas Clapham, Leeds, Excursion Manager; or the Leeds Royal Gardens.

109

Tommy Clapham's advertisement for the Gardens, now called Leeds Royal Gardens, from White's 1853 Directory of Leeds. The entry charges had been reduced and the emphasis shifted to entertainment. The new train line through Burley Park Station served the Gardens, making access easier for people living outside Leeds. *(Thoresby Society)*

Public Gardens in England', and military bands, elaborate fireworks, and hot-air balloon ascents by an 'intrepid aeronaut' were among the attractions advertised. The emphasis had shifted from education and improvement to entertainment. Every opportunity was seized to bring customers into the Gardens. When Leeds, along with the whole country, was celebrating the news of the final fall of Sebastopol in September 1855, with all the streets brilliantly illuminated after dark by gas jets and coloured 'transparencies' in the shops, and by candles in all the house windows, Tommy Clapham advertised that a whole ox would be roasted in the Gardens and portions distributed to everyone there, the band would play, and the Gardens would be specially illuminated to mark the occasion.[12]

But even he could not make the Gardens a success. He advertised that they could be hired for private occasions provided these were not 'of an immoral nature', but this did not help. They were finally closed and dismantled in 1858. He subsequently bought land next to Woodhouse Moor, including a cricket ground, and opened the Royal Park Gardens, which featured a dancing platform, skating rink, clay pigeon-shooting and other amusements, but these too closed some years later, and now only the local street names retain their memory.

The former bear pit in Cardigan Road: people climbed the towers to throw buns to the bear in the pit below. The building was left derelict and filled with rubbish after the Gardens closed; it was acquired and restored by Leeds Civic Trust in 1966. The original aim to display a range of wild animals in enclosures in the Gardens had to be abandoned at an early stage for lack of money (and perhaps enough enthusiasm).

---

12. *Leeds Mercury*, 18.9.1855. The long and gruelling siege of Sebastopol in the Crimea by French and British troops had lasted almost a year and had cost many lives.

DEVELOPMENT

Meanwhile the Headingley 'Old Gardens', as they were called, were developed for building. The lakes were filled in and the site was opened up by the construction of Cardigan Road through the centre, creating a new link between Headingley and Burley and with two new roads planned to join it, Bainbrigge Road, and St Michael's Lane.[13] The spacious plots on either side of Cardigan Road were offered for sale for 'Villa residences', and restrictive covenants were imposed to ensure that only appropriately grand houses were erected. The purchasers included John Hepper, the auctioneer and estate agent; Henry Ludolf, flax and wool merchant, who bought several plots with a view to developing them; and other wealthy businessmen from the town. The houses were individually designed and several well-known Leeds architects were involved, notably George Corson, who designed 'Manor Court', and 'Clareville' for John Hepper. Many of these fine Victorian villas still stand along Cardigan Road and, although much altered, retain some of their grandeur.

It is still possible to get a sense of the old Gardens by walking down Spring Road, crossing Cardigan Road to see the imposing high stone walls which flanked the entrance, and then following the wall, largely unbroken, along Chapel Lane down to Burley Park Station, where the old Lodge building next to the Burley entrance to the Gardens remained into the 1980s. Here people left the train to enter the peaceful greenery of the Gardens and escape the smoke and stench of the town, and later the families of the wealthy enjoyed their exclusive leafy suburb. Now the traffic roars along Cardigan Road and the environment looks very different, but the 'habitation of the bear' remains as a reminder of the past, and some of the gardens, for example the spacious garden of Cardigan House, have kept the walks, trees, shrubs and perhaps a little of the atmosphere of the old Botanical Gardens.

---

13. Martin & Fenwick, *Plan of Headingley Gardens Estate*, not dated but c. 1868, WYAS Leeds, WYL160/55.

A HEALTHY PLACE?

During the nineteenth century Headingley enjoyed the reputation of being one of the healthiest areas of Leeds to live in, and even in the 1890s, when it had become much more crowded, the Headingley ward still had the lowest death rate in the city.[14] The sanitary condition of Leeds had been a source of deep concern for most of the century, and in spite of major improvements in sewerage and water supply and the clearance of many of the worst slum areas, its death rate in the final years of the century was exceeded only by Liverpool and Manchester, and over a fifth of babies died before their first birthday. While conditions in Headingley were good, given its position high above the river away from the smoke and polluted air, with a plentiful natural supply of water from springs and wells, it did not entirely escape the problems so rampant elsewhere.

In 1862, a major row broke out over a Council proposal to link Headingley to the main sewerage system: there were accusations of 'filthy' cesspits on Headingley Hill poisoning wells and polluting the river, and counter arguments from residents anxious not to pay higher rates, insisting that Headingley could manage its own drainage system perfectly well using the river and Meanwood Beck.[15] However, the need for proper sewerage became increasingly obvious, and by the 1880s most of Headingley was connected to the main system. But problems still arose over the collection and disposal of night soil from privies and rubbish from ashpits: in 1883 there were complaints about offensive smells from night soil and rubbish deposited as manure on the fields at the end of Grove Lane, near Oakfield Terrace, which aroused the concern of the Medical Officer of Health. Some of the new back-to-back housing being built in Headingley also failed to reach adequate sanitary standards: problems with drainage and sewerage in the Highburys and the Granbys had to be investigated by the Medical Officer in 1895/6.

While Headingley mostly escaped the worst of the various outbreaks of cholera in the town, it experienced its own epidemic of typhoid fever in July 1889.[16] At first it was thought that this might have been caused by an escape of 'sewer gas' after dry weather, but it quickly became evident that the problem was contaminated milk supplied to residents of Headingley and Woodhouse by the White House Farm at Meanwood. 'Disease and death at twopence a pint' was the *Mercury's* headline. The Medical Officer of Health visited the farm to investigate, but failed to take action or to halt the supply of milk until a week later. 153 people contracted typhoid and of these 15 died. As a result the Medical Officer resigned, and there was a call for the position to be better paid in order to attract better qualified candidates for this important post. The epidemic triggered a further debate on the urgent need for improvements in sanitary arrangements in the town and helped to hasten remedial action.[17]

---

14. See *Leeds Sanitary Committee Reports, 1883–1913*, and the annual *Reports of the Leeds Medical Officer of Health*, 1895–97, (Leeds Local Studies Library).

15. Case for the Opinion of Counsel, 31.1.1862, and Report of Discussion in the Leeds Town Council on Headingley Drainage, 10.4.1862 (Leeds Local Studies Library, LP352.63H342 and L352.63L517).

16. Reported in the *Leeds Mercury* from 6.7.1889 to 10.8.1889, and discussed in *Fit and Proper Persons*, by E.P.Hennock, London, 1973.

17. In place of the old deep ashpits from which rubbish had to be dug out and carted away, a 'tub' to hold the week's rubbish, to be emptied weekly, was suggested – the origin of the dustbin. The benefits of water closets or dry earth closets were argued for, instead of the old wet middens, many of which were still in use and indeed were still being allowed in new buildings by the Town Council's Building Clauses Committee, in opposition to the views of the Sanitary Committee.

FISH AND CHIPS — AND NORTH LANE

BRETT'S FISH AND Chips shop and restaurant, housed in this ivy-clad stone cottage with its colourful garden in front full of flowers, has been a Headingley landmark for as long as anyone can remember. It was just after the First World War, almost 90 years ago, that Arthur Brett bought this cottage in North Lane, moved his home there from Bennett Road, and set up his new business of selling fried fish and chips – bound to find plenty of takers in this rapidly expanding suburb with its new close-packed terrace housing nearby. The cottage he bought had a longer history, dating back to the 1850s, part of the story of the development of North Lane, the old narrow lane which curved round the northern fringe of the village, linking Kirkstall Lane with the roads to Otley and across Headingley Moor to Monk Bridge.

FISH AND CHIPS

Members of the Brett family first came to Headingley around 1899 from Rastrick and settled in the newly-built Trelawn Terrace. The rapid growth of the village offered good work opportunities and attracted incomers. Arthur Brett worked first in the family joinery firm,[1] and then acquired a horse and cart and set up as a carting agent, offering his services to ferry people and their baggage around, help them move house, and fetch and carry loads of coal or other heavy goods. In 1921 he launched a new venture selling fish and chips, founding an enterprise which nearly a century later still bears his name.

Every day he drove with his horse and cart down to Leeds fish market and brought back fresh fish for his shop. His two horses were stabled next door at the end of Wellfield Place, reached by steps over the wall. As time went on, he was accompanied by his young son, Charlie, who learnt the business at his side. They expanded, in the 1930s taking over the two cottages next door to live in, and creating space for a restaurant through the shop. Ever popular, the shop was open for long hours – during the Second World War till one in the morning, to serve the many late night workers. In due course Charlie ('Charles on Sunday,' he liked to joke) took over the business and continued to run it for many years, a familiar figure in his long white apron, always ready with a cheery greeting, still fondly remembered by many of his former customers.

Charlie Brett and his brother Jack were both motorcycle enthusiasts and racers, winning top prizes in the Isle of Man TT races – indeed Jack was well-known on the international circuit. The yard behind the cottage used to echo to the noise of their bikes revving up, causing complaints from the neighbours, rudely woken from their morning slumber. But it was through cricket that Brett's became most well-known. The queues outside were extra long when the matches were on, and many of the players themselves were devoted customers.[2] One of Charlie's fondest memories from the 1930s and 40s was of the great Yorkshire and England batsman, the immaculate, Brylcreemed Herbert Sutcliffe, parking his Rolls Royce outside and coming in for his customary order, which included two fish for his dogs. In the 1970s John Arlott, the BBC cricket correspondent, was persuaded to try Brett's; he was won over, and wrote an article for the *Guardian* wine column (he was their wine correspondent too) singing its praises. A copy still hangs on the wall in Brett's. From then on during every Test Match he came for his meal with members of the England cricket team, and when he retired he took it over for a whole evening for his farewell party. He remained in affectionate contact with Charlie Brett for the rest of his life.

Ill health finally forced Charlie, very unwillingly, to retire. Although the shop and restaurant are now under separate management, the Brett name has been preserved, the cottage retains all its charm, and Charlie Brett's daughter, Jane, continues to own the terrace, living next door and taking care of the wonderful garden, a small oasis amid the traffic and an example of continuity and stability in the midst of the now increasingly transient population of Headingley.

BRETT'S COTTAGE

The cottage Arthur Brett bought in 1921 was in fact two small houses knocked into one, part of a row of four (12–18 North Lane) built in the 1850s, when North Lane was still semi-rural. The land it was built on, like most of the surrounding land, had belonged to Lord Cardigan, the Lord of the Manor, and had been rented out to a local farmer. In 1850 the Cardigan estate decided to sell off part of its land in Headingley, and a two-day auction was organised in October. Many of the plots offered for sale were on Headingley Moor, land which had been allotted to Lord Cardigan in the 1834 enclosure, but some of the fields which bordered North Lane and elsewhere in the village were included. The auction was not a success and much of the land remained unsold, but a few of the smaller plots in the village did find buyers, one of them this plot on North Lane (Lot 50).[3]

The land had been part of a field called House Close, rented from the Cardigan estate for grazing by a farmer, Thomas Musgrove. The buyer was George Bailey, a stonemason from Far Headingley,[4] and it looks as though he bought the land for investment and built the cottages to rent out. Perhaps he foresaw that as Headingley expanded as a residential area for the town, more low-cost housing would be needed for all the people providing services for the occupants of the new mansions and villas: gardeners and laundresses, small shopkeepers, dressmakers and milliners, joiners and quarrymen working in the local

1. Saunders & Brett, advertised in the *Headingley Directory and Almanac*, 1905.

2. An affectionate memoir of Charlie Brett and the attractions of Brett's is included in *Fred Trueman's Yorkshire* by Fred Trueman and Don Mosey, Stanley Paul, London, 1984.

3. The two neighbouring lots, 49 and 51, were also sold, both to local men. The houses in Wellfield Place (Lot 49) were built by 1872; the three tall brick houses on the other side of Bretts (Lot 51) were built later, in the mid 1880s, rather incongruously joined on to this low row of stone cottages.

quarries, which were busy producing stone for all the building in progress around the village and in the town. And so it proved. In 1882, for example, two of the cottages were occupied by women working as laundresses, another by a dressmaker and one by a gardener;[5] and in 1887 John Lupton of Moorlands in Alma Road (where the Lupton flats now stand) bought two of the cottages to provide a permanent home for his gardener, an arrangement which continued into the 1930s.[6]

The cottages were modest: originally one main room on each floor, and an ashpit privy outside in the yard, shared with the adjoining house. They had the luxury of fresh water, as a watercourse (one of many in the village) ran under the yard to the well in Wellfield Place next door, and water could be fetched up through a manhole (it is still there). And in front they had their distinctive long gardens down to North Lane, still a feature today. Perhaps it was the availability of fresh water and the good gardens for drying which meant that many of the tenants over the years worked as laundresses, taking in washing from the larger houses around, where the mistress could afford to 'give out' her heavy weekly washing.[7] Doing other people's laundry was a useful occupation for women on low incomes and there were many, particularly widows, offering this service in the village.

4. His name is still to be found in Far Headingley, in Back Bailey's Place. The Conveyance to him of Lot 50 was dated 30.12.1850 (W. R. Registry of Deeds, QT p.506).

5. *McCorquodale's Post Office Directory of Leeds*, 1882.

6.Indenture of 1.6.1887, W.R. Registry of Deeds, 1887, Vol.15, p.895.

7. Mrs Beeton comments that many households, even in the suburbs where the houses have gardens, send out their washing, though often 'the fine linen, cottons and muslins are washed at home, even where the bulk of the washing is given out.' (*Book of Household Management*, 1861).

Westfield Grove, on the corner of North Lane and St Michael's Road. This fine pair of semi-detached houses was built in 1844 by the Leeds printer Reid Newsome. One of the first tenants was Richard Oastler, the renowned champion of factory reform and campaigner for the poor. He came to live here on his release from prison for debt in 1844 and stayed two years in this rural corner of Headingley, 'this lovely spot' as he called it.

NORTH LANE IN THE 1830S AND 40S

Before the sales of land in the 1850s, North Lane was like a country lane, very narrow in places, with fields and gardens on both sides, a scatter of cottages all at odd angles, and a few small local businesses.[8] There was a farm on the bend where Ash Road now joins North Lane, and the old farmhouse there, known as Ivy Cottage, still survives in Cross Chapel Street. Further on, where the Lounge and the Arc stand now, there was a tannery with a tall chimney and in front of it the owner's house and garden. This tannery, run by Thomas Shipley since 1824, had been in existence since the 1780s and perhaps earlier; it was still working in 1851, when it employed six men.[9] Behind it, (where Harris's Greengrocers is now) stood a house and cottage with a malt kiln, used in the brewing process.

---

8. As shown in the 1831 Enclosure Sale Plan; 1846 Tithe Map and Schedule; and the 1851 Census (H.O.107/2315/302). It looks as though this area of North Lane had long had an association with business rather than just farming: when land here was sold in 1689 the sale included a 'leadhouse' (containing a vat), suggesting either brewing or dying cloth (there was a field called ' tenter close' nearby, so the latter seems more likely).

9. The tannery was built on land sold by Thomas Brown to Samuel Waddington in 1775; Samuel's will of 1784 refers to the tanyard; his grandson Tommis sold it to Thomas Shipley in 1824 (Marshall Deeds, WYAS Leeds, WYL160/68). In 1851 Thomas Shipley and Son were trading as leather merchants at 20 Salem Place in Leeds.

The malting business belonged to the Thompsons, a long-established Headingley family who had bought land along North Lane in the eighteenth century;[10] it was still in operation in 1839 but had fallen out of use by 1850, and a few years later the malt kiln and ancillary buildings were demolished and replaced by a row of four houses, Grove Place (these survived until 1931). On the other side of the Lane, there was a market garden and nursery where William Mellish, gardener and seedsman, employed four men in 1851. And at the corner where North Lane joined Otley Road, Thomas Duffield the blacksmith had his workshop, next to a little cluster of cottages.

At the bottom of North Lane, on one side (where South Parade is now) a long gated carriage drive, with a small house for the gatekeeper, led up through parkland to Headingley House and Headingley Lodge (see p.139). Opposite, on the corner of North Lane and St Michael's Road, two fine stone houses, still surviving today, were built in 1844 by Reid Newsome, who ran a stationery, printing and bookselling business in town, at one time in partnership with the brother of Edward Baines of the *Leeds Mercury*. Having lived in Headingley for some years, Reid Newsome decided to buy some land to build a house for himself, and he chose this corner plot, originally part of the village common land ('the low green'),[11] with a row of old cottages behind, on the edge of the fields. In this pleasant spot, looking down the wooded hillside towards the river, he built a pair of semi-detached houses, one for himself and one to rent out. He called them Westfield Grove. His first tenant, from 1844 to 1846, was a well-known and controversial figure: Richard Oastler, the famous agitator for factory reform, freshly released from prison where he had spent almost four years for debt, and now trying to re-establish himself back near Leeds, the town of his birth.

---

10. The Thompson family and their connection with brewing can be traced back to the early eighteenth century.

11. His purchase became the subject of dispute with the Cardigan estate over the rights of the Lord of the Manor in this piece of former common land (WYAS Leeds, RDP39/131).

RICHARD OASTLER (1789–1861)

Richard Oastler, the 'Factory King', fought passionately for the reform of working conditions in the factories and mills, particularly for the young children who worked appallingly long hours. 'Yorkshire Slavery' was how he famously described the life of these poor children. He led the campaign for shorter working hours, the 'Ten Hours' movement, and took on the role of spokesman for the poor and oppressed, fervently opposing the introduction of the new Poor Law of 1834. His violent oratory and inflammatory political activities brought him into conflict with his employer: he was dismissed from his post as steward at Fixby Hall, accused of debt and imprisoned until money could be found to settle the claims against him. During almost four years in prison, mainly in the Fleet, he published a regular and widely-read journal known as the Fleet Papers, arguing his case on the social issues dear to his heart. Meanwhile his loyal supporters collected and borrowed money to buy his freedom, and he was finally released from prison in early 1844. They had hoped to raise enough money to give him a pension so that he could continue his political campaigning, but instead he had to find work to support himself and his family. In July 1844 he came to live in Westfield Grove, Headingley, 'this lovely spot' as he called it,[12] happy to be with his wife and adopted daughter again after his years of imprisonment. There he set up as a sharebroker, a partner in Wellbeloved and Oastler, sharebrokers, Headingley.[13] What caused him to come to Headingley to live and work is not clear, but he was not to stay very long. Sadly his beloved wife Mary died just a year later in June 1845, aged only 52. She was buried at St Stephen's Church, Kirkstall, the church they had attended, and their two children who had died in infancy were reinterred with her. Perhaps her death prompted his move back to London in 1846, where he had been offered other work. The Ten Hour Act was finally passed in 1847, hailed as his crowning achievement. He died in 1861 on a return visit to Yorkshire, and was buried in a vault at St Stephen's, next to his wife and children. Thousands of work-people turned out for his funeral, and it was reported that 'even stern manhood' was moved to tears at the loss of their spokesman and hero.[14]

---

12. *Fleet Papers*: 10 August 1844.

13. Listed in *Williams's Directory of the Borough of Leeds*, 1845.

In the 1850 Cardigan sale, Reid Newsome, who was still living in Westfield Grove, bought the adjoining plot of land (lot 57) along St Michael's Road (then still called Kirkstall Road), perhaps to protect himself from unwelcome neighbours. It became part of the Westfield Nursery garden which extended behind the houses on North Lane, with flower and vegetable beds, trees and glasshouses, until the end of the century. The plot next door (Lot 56) was bought by John Eyres, a wealthy grocer, tea dealer and importer of foreign fruit with a business in town in Upper Head Row, and there he built himself a large house, set back in a spacious garden, which he called 'Bleak House'. Clearly a Charles Dickens enthusiast, he assumed others would know that the fictional Bleak House is in fact not at all bleak but uniquely warm and welcoming.[15] John Eyres left around 1870, and the house was occupied in the later nineteenth century by various merchants with businesses in town, and during the following century, much altered, was used for a range of purposes: a youth club, a Friends' Meeting House, and from the 1970s a British Legion centre. It now houses the New Headingley Club.

MORE SALES – CHAPEL STREET, BENNETT ROAD, AND THE PUMPING STATION

When the first auction of land in 1850 failed to find many buyers, the Cardigan estate had to devise a new strategy.

---

14. The *Leeds Mercury* of 29.8.1861 has a full account of his funeral. His grave at St Stephen's Kirkstall is difficult to see as it is behind a grille under the church. The inscription reads 'He rests from his labours and his works do follow him'. There is a memorial window to him in the church, from his adopted daughter. His statue was erected in Bradford in 1861, paid for by public subscription; and in 1925 a memorial tablet was put up in Leeds Parish Church. For more information on Oastler's life and work see C. Driver, *Tory Radical: The Life of Richard Oastler*, Oxford, 1946 (though this does not mention his brief time in Headingley).

15. Charles Dickens' novel *Bleak House* was published in 1852. In 1858, around the time this house was being built, Dickens himself visited Leeds to give public readings from his works, to great acclaim.

'Bleak House', now the New Headingley Club, St Michael's Road built around 1858 by John Eyres, a wealthy grocer, tea dealer and importer of foreign fruit with a business in town.

The Cardigan agent in Headingley, George Hayward, worked out a plan to subdivide the large plots into much smaller ones, and designated a number of new access roads which would make the land easier to develop for residential use and attractive to the small investor. These new roads, numbered but not named on the plan, included the roads we now know as Chapel Street and Chapel Place, and Bennett Road on the other side of North Lane.[16] A second auction was held in May 1851 and this time there was much more interest. The small plots along Chapel Street were sold and over the next few years the small stone terraces we see today, a mix of through and back-to-back houses, were built, each with at least some small garden area to soften the stone landscape. The unique and charming Chapel Square, with its central archway off Chapel Street, is a feature of this development.[17]

---

16. 1851 Sale Plan, WYAS Leeds, WYL160/M719.

17. About the same time, Alma Cottages with their distinctive castellated outside privies were built on the narrow strip of land behind Chapel Square. This piece of land had been acquired by William Beckett of New Grange in the course of the 1834 enclosure, apparently for an access road into his estate. It was still described as a road in 1847, but by 1861 these eight cottages had been built, presumably by the Becketts (there is no record of a sale to anyone else in this period.) The road was originally gated at the Otley Road end.

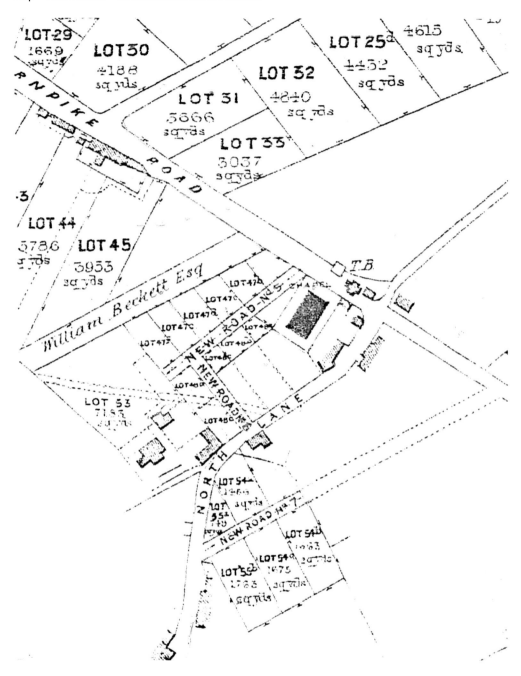

An extract from the sale plan of Cardigan land auctioned on 26 and 28 May 1851. This is a revised version of the earlier (1850) plan and divides the land into much smaller plots, with proposed new roads to facilitate development: road no. 5 became Chapel Street, no. 6 Chapel Place, no. 7 Bennett Road. Some plots had already been sold in 1850, including the plot in North Lane where Brett's row of cottages was built. (West Yorkshire Archive Service, Leeds, WYL160/M719)

Across North Lane, three plots of land, part of a field called Well Close which backed onto the newly planned Bennett Road, were bought in 1859 from their original purchasers by the Leeds Corporation Waterworks, for the erection of a pumping station (this is the building which is now the Taps public house). Headingley was a natural choice for this new development. Since 1843, the water supply for the whole town of Leeds had come through Headingley, brought from Eccup reservoir through the Blackmoor Tunnel, the Seven Arches aqueduct[18] and Weetwood to Headingley, then on to the reservoir on Woodhouse Moor.[19] The Corporation had taken over control of the water supply in 1852, after much heart-searching, the main advocate of public ownership being John Hope Shaw of Shaw House, Headingley, then in one of his three periods of office as Mayor. It quickly became evident to the newly-formed Waterworks Committee that it would be necessary to install equipment to pump water to the higher level areas where the town was now expanding: initially Bramley, later Chapeltown, then further out still. The site in North Lane was bought, and the foundation stone of the new pumping station was laid in 1858, as recorded on a tablet still in place on the wall. It opened in 1860, a handsome stone building, its distinctive height and tall curving twin gables a symbol of the Corporation's pride in its mission to provide clean water for its citizens. The first pump was powered by steam, and later more pumps were added until by 1911 the station had a pumping capacity of almost 20,000,000 gallons a day. Originally a tall chimney stood at its front (where the entrance porch is now), visible from far away, but this was demolished around 1928 when electricity took over from steam, and no sign of it now remains. The building was

18. Still to be seen in Adel woods; it was abandoned in 1866 when a new cast iron main was built.

19. A useful account is given in the brochure *Leeds Corporation Waterworks Undertaking, 1852–1952 Centenary* (Thoresby Society). See also Derek Fraser, ed., *A History of Modern Leeds*, Chapter XII, Section III.

decommissioned in the 1980s and in 1994 was converted into the current public house.[20]

THE CHANGING SCENE

Around 1860 the old North Lane tannery closed, like many small domestic enterprises no longer viable in comparison with new large-scale industrialised businesses. Its chimney was demolished, providing an exciting spectacle for local onlookers, and the site seems then to have remained undeveloped for many years, its buildings

The pumping station in North Lane (now the 'Taps' public house), opened in 1860, designed to pump water to the higher level areas into which the town was expanding. Originally its pumps were powered by steam and a high chimney stood in front, demolished in the late 1920s. The base of the old chimney can still be seen in this photograph from c1950, when the station was still in use. *(Thoresby Society)*

20. The building is listed, and its conversion was subject to a number of conditions. Some of the old pumping machinery still remains underground (thanks to Paul Stephenson, the manager, for this information).